Diana an English rose

Diana

An English rose

Susan Maxwell Skinner & Anwar Hussein

Illustrations: Marialuisa Marino

N INDICATION of the magnitude of an event is that most people can remember where they were and what they were doing when they heard the news. By those criteria, the dreadful accident in that underpass in Paris in the early hours of August 31, 1997, ranks with the assassination of President John F Kennedy in 1963, for most of the world. Whatever part Diana, Princess of Wales, had played in people's lives and thoughts before she and Dodi Al Fayed were killed, there was a universal feeling that the world had lost something special, something good, something irreplaceable. At Royalty magazine, which had chronicled the rise and transformation of the gauche young ingenue from "Shy Di" to the rank of icon and certainly role model for a generation, our feelings were as intense as any. Now, a year after those dreadful events, it is a pleasure to contribute to a book which, I feel, genuinely shows the most compelling and compassionate insight – in both words and pictures – of the woman whose life touched millions worldwide. The definitive portrait of Diana, Princess of Wales, may be still some way off in the future, but Susan Maxwell Skinner, framed by Anwar Hussein's superb photo-journalism, has taken a big step in that direction.

Bob Houston, Founding Editor, Royalty.

The author acknowledges input (from as far back as 1982) from Palace aides including Michael Shea, Warwick Hutchings, Frances Cornish, the late Steven Barry and the late Victor Chapman. Thanks also to milliners John Boyd and Frederick Fox, hairdresser Kevin Shanley, designers David Sassoon and Belinda Belville. My praise to the Ninth Earl Spencer, for no serious study of the Princess of Wales could be complete without researching the precious material in the Diana Museum at Althorp, Northhamptonshire. The value of this material to historians cannot be overrated. My gratitude particularly goes to Diana's voice coach and actor Peter Settelen, for insight into his remarkable student. Further help came came from my photographer friend Jayne Fincher and from veteran royal pictureman Anwar Hussein. Special praise is due to my dear friends Susan Samois (in London) and Maria Egloff (in California) for research assistance. Tom Egloff and Tom Charlesworth gave computer help. And lastly, thanks to my husband John Skinner, for his enthusiasm, and for the hours he spent improving my computer skills.

L'EPPI PUBLICATIONS

P.O. Box 3278,
805 Finchley Road,
London NW11 8DP.
Tel. +44(0)1814580167

FIRST PUBLISHED IN THE UNITED KINGDOM 1998 LEPPI PUBLICATIONS ■ BRITISH LIBRARY CATALOGUING IN PUBLICATION DATA ■ LEPPI PUBLICATIONS ■ DIANA, AN ENGLISH ROSE ■ ISBN 095216441■ © 1998 Leppi Publications, Savonarola Inc ■ Printed in Italy

PHOTOGRAPH CREDITS: ANWAR HUSSEIN, HULTON GETTY LIBRARY, REX FEATURES, UK PRESS

Contents

You bring light to people's lives

Mother Theresa, 1992

On a summer's day in 1981, we married Diana Spencer to the Prince of Wales. The Archbishop of Canterbury was there, of course. But by "we" I mean "we the public", who had taken her to our hearts and wanted her in our lives forever. I also mean "we the press", who had plucked a 19 year-old from obscurity and raised her so high that current events without Diana seemed unthinkable. By much the same process, on a summer's day sixteen years later, we buried her. Between time we let her – just as she let herself – become the centre of not just a global industry, but of our fantasies. Through her, we could dream the impossible dream – to be beloved, beautiful, famous, rich and no matter how many dainty dishes were set before us, thin, thin, thin.

When it became clear that the fairy tale bride was unhappily married, that she suffered from eating disorders and clinical depression, our fantasies contrived a sad heroine. When she lost her title and was snubbed by the establishment, we had a rebel heroine. When she died and it seemed her in-laws were not mourning sufficiently, we hailed a martyred heroine. We since have had time to consider our feelings. Perhaps in decrying Windsor reserve, we felt less guilty for our part in loving this poor woman to death.

Mario Testino, Diana's friend and the photographer she chose for some of her last portraits, considers her loss a hard lesson to society in general. "We are all implicated in the invasion (of Diana's privacy)," he said after the funeral. "It comes from a desire to have more and more of something we crave . . . that wonderful smile and the allure she possessed. All of us demanded this invasion."

It continues. At the Spencer family seat of Althorp, a mock-Greek temple is now Diana's monument. Open to the public for two months in 1998, it was daily seen by thousands of pilgrims. If we expected emotional catharsis at Diana's home, tears were rare. Visitors laid bouquets, pondered relics in the Diana museum and, generally, smiled from ear to ear. Inspired at least for the length of the visit, we tried to be kinder to each other, as we imagine Diana would have wished.

Her incredible funeral is now a memory but we still cannot get enough of Diana's legend. In the light of scorn by at least one Anglican archbishop for the lingering "cult of Diana," the displays at Althorp were masterpieces of political correctness. If the lakeside shrine has a pagan look, Charles Spencer cleverly Christianised it by attaching a golden cross to the roof's apex.

November 1987. Diana meets the people during a seven day visit to West Germany.
(Facing page) August 1987. Charles and Diana enjoyed a third successive holiday as guests of the Spanish Royal Family in Marivent Palace outside Palma on the island of Majorca – Diana with Prince Harry.
(Previous page) Diana and Mother Theresa in New York. Their first meeting was in Calcutta in February 1992. Mother Theresa died on September 5, 1997, only five days after Diana.

Amidst the ebullience of visitors – camaraderie was cemented as we queued by Althorp's gates before 10am – I had to remind myself that we came to see monuments to a woman whom we felt was family. We clattered noisily over the cobblestones, bought ice-cream and lined up to learn more about our icon, from relics and from amateur films of her earliest days. These fractured flickers proved what Diana only hinted at in childhood recollections. We felt her beautiful mother's ambivalence to yet another girl-child as a third Spencer daughter was christened. We saw an infant who learned to be the world's most photogenic woman through sheer necessity. To pose coquettishly, to dance and dive were foolproof ways for Diana to get attention from a camera-mad father. We marvelled at what a brilliant dancer and actress she was, even as a child. We felt the stoic acceptance of a divorced kid, packed off with her tuck box to yet another boarding school. Also in the exhibition, we read school reports that confirmed the rotten time she had during her education – a pathetic seventeen per cent in her 1973 maths examination – and we saw her means of escape from inferiority, the tattered pink ballet *pointes*.

Yet Charles Spencer took care that we should not feel sorry for his sister. The videos and pictures of a grown-up princess did not suggest Diana's heartaches.

Watching her busy career as a mother and a humanitarian, we felt only her fulfillment. Displays of her gowns cheered us with glittering rainbows of sequins. We remembered how excitingly she sparkled and shone before she was gone. However briefly, this style and her smile made our lives happier. Her brother chose to underscore this phenomenon, just as in his famous funeral eulogy (which he displayed in its handwritten draft at Althorp), he thanked Diana "for the way you brightened our lives".

On most days of the two-month Diana-fest at Althorp, the young Earl was very visible. Tall and attractive, with the same blue eyes his sister had mesmerised the world with, he was the only living link to Diana on the premises. We pilgrims mobbed him. In the year since her death, Charles Spencer had been tossed by a storm of public opinion. At The Funeral, he was the most admired man in Britain. His incisive eulogy was likened to the Gettysburg Address for historical import. But within weeks, nasty details of his divorce re-invented him as a blue-blooded Blue Beard. His popularity fell to its lowest ebb as 1998 progressed, when he battled with Diana's trust fund and was accused of profiting by his famous sister.

As Althorp opened on July 1, he initiated his own public relations defensive. Not through the press but through the 2,500 people who swarmed to his ancestral digs every day. He assumed a ploy that was pure-Diana. Westminster Abbey's angry young Earl was now the caring, sharing people's peer. As if sensing the divinity thrust upon him, Lord Spencer knelt and talked to the handicapped. He touched hands and faces and looked deeply into our eyes. However sceptically I had arrived at the estate in the first days of July, I found myself thanking him for sharing his house and his time with the masses. "Oh, it's only for two months," he smiled. The implication was that his sister could never close her gates and retreat at the end of summer. Death was her only escape from the public magnifying glass. And even then, her sons and the Spencers would share her grave with the rest of the world. Diana's mother had to cast her mind back to "the nine months before she was born" to think of a time when Diana was "completely mine".

In death – when her name was used to raise about £50 million pounds in one year and to sell such products as margarine – just as in almost half of her bizarre life, the princess remained the People's Property. In the words of lyricist Tim Rice (describing another 20th-century superstar) she was "a diamond in their dull, grey lives".

A diamond . . . but what a diamond! Diana and Charles were dancing at a gala in Sydney in 1983 and, like everyone else at the ball, I was bowled over by her brilliance. I recall the glittering turquoise dress, the priceless necklace, the silver belt and shoes. But most of all, how Diana herself glittered. As she pivoted wildly, I could hear her giggling *joie de vivre*. Her teeth, eyes and hair all caught the spotlight

Sydney, Australia 1983. A social event at the Wentworth Hotel where Charles and Diana danced the night away. (Facing page) Melbourne, Australia 1985. Swirling around the dance floor with Charles. In a silk dress by Bruce Oldfield, Diana chose to wear the Queen Mary choker as a headband. She looked happy but there were already a few cracks in her marriage and she looked very thin.

1982. A pregnant Diana in Windsor. Right up to her confinement, the Princess chose to accompany her husband to Polo at weekends (Facing page) 1982. Diana, casually dressed in dungarees in Cowdray Park. In those days Diana's expression revealed the unwordliness of a girl not yet twenty. She was going into marriage with all the willingness in the world to make a good wife and a future queen, but she could never have imagined how great the task and challenge that her married life would turn out to be.

and it seemed that no more magical person inhabited the planet than this 21 year-old. I remember the song the band played: "The More I See You." Like the rest of the world, I had seen a lot of her. Even at that absurd age, she had been a deity for years.

I had been at the Wedding of the Century. I waited at St Mary's Hospital for two days and watched Diana take her first-born home. It was my job to learn who designed every gown in her wardrobe. I knew the origin of every diamond she wore. In time, I would travel all over the world with her. I saw her excitement as she launched a huge ocean liner, her nervousness meeting presidents and her compassion as she touched the untouchables. I felt her heartache as she relinquished her sons' hands on their first days at school. Like everyone else on the planet, I felt she had grown up before my eyes: from blushing teenager, to focused parent and later to take on the woes of the world as humanitarian activist. It was

only inevitable, I suppose, that I should watch her funeral and, eleven months later, visit her memorial at Althorp.

Like everyone else, I knew she could be moody and controlling – that such foibles caused her brother Charles to brand Diana "unique," "complex" and "standing tall enough not to need to be seen as a saint". People who loved her knew the pressure she felt and excused her caprices. From a press point of view they hardly mattered. She was, after all, superstar of the entire global road show. So she could make – and change – the rules at whim. As she peaked in confidence, you felt her sensual presence before you saw her. India Hicks, one of Diana's bridesmaids, called it "something to do with star quality; she walked into a room and you knew she had arrived without any fanfare or announcement." Diana was so much larger than life that, at her death, her history flashed before us in banner headlines: "Fairy tale Bride", "Devoted Mother", "Angel of Compassion", "Saint", "Sinner", "Loose Cannon", "Betrayed Wife", "Gay Divorceé", "Queen of Hearts". And, at long last, "Princess In Love". Unashamedly and mercifully in love, even as she drew her last breath.

To observers, she lived at breathtaking speed. Her brother Charles marvelled at the "boundless energy which (she) could barely contain." The childhood films at Althorp confirm what so many of us remember. A lithe girl who ran, skipped and danced, who seldom walked and found it impossible to sit still. As she neared her end, the pace was manic; a race against time. Diana's speech coach, Peter Settelen, told me "She was someone in a hurry. I believe she knew she didn't have that long to live and do the work she was sent to do."

Six years her senior, I did not expect to outlive the teenager in yellow dungarees whom I first met before her wedding at a polo match. But I treasure that image from one night in Sydney – like diamonds – forever. Diana spinning faster and faster. Hardly more than a child. Giggling and flashing in the spotlight. A fabled, fairy thing . . . except she was mortal like the rest of us and after sixteen busy, glittering years, the spotlight had consumed her.

Before Diana's funeral, the Queen told a grieving world: "There are lessons to be learned from her life and the extraordinary and moving reaction to her death . . . " One lesson was that a Princess – with one foot in the mystique of royalty and another in the intrigue of show business – was on very dangerous ground. And though it fascinated us to see her balancing her weight so brilliantly, in time she paid the price . . . horribly.

But had she lived through years more of controversial love affairs, marriages, more divorces (for she was not easy to live with) and the decline of her beauty, society would perhaps have grown cynical about its princess. Her funeral – in the year 2000 and something – might have been a minor and depressing event. As it was, through such a premature death, the aura she had magically generated in

The Princess of Wales wearing a stunning seven strand choker necklace.
(Facing page) April 18, 1989. At a function in aid of the British Lung Foundation. Diana in a black dress and a red jacket by Catherine Walker.

sixteen years remained untarnished, intact into the afterlife. It cheered us that if our heroine had to exit our lives, she did so while happy, beautiful and in love. A psychologist in far-off New Zealand told me of speaking to children about death; almost every child wanted to be "with Diana". It can be a blessed thing for the candle to burn out, as Sir Elton John said, so long before the legend.

Several days after the funeral, Diana's mother rowed herself to Diana's Island at Althorp and made some sense of the whole Diana tragedy. "As I rowed back," Mrs Shand Kydd told a Catholic mass in Scotland, "I noticed a thin covering of weed on the water, cut in two by the boat. I looked back and saw it join like a curtain . . . I could feel my beloved Diana was at peace. Her earthly life was short but complete. I knew then that all she had to do was completed – that all was well. Very well."

(Facing page) Diana and Charles toured India in 1992. The press devoted much of their time to following Diana, who had separate engagements. In Hyderabad at Lallapet High School, this exotically dressed little girl befriended the Princess.

Remember,
you're a Spencer!

Diana, spurring herself on 1997

So much has changed. Yet so much remains the same. The passing of Althorp's most famous daughter altered the mood of a planet. It re-invented the style of a monarchy. It dulled trade in a nation of shopkeepers. It perfumed an entire city. And for one funereal day, it almost stopped the world. But Althorp House in Northamptonshire has weathered five hundred years of changes. Still it casts the same Elizabethan shadows over the very sheep pastures that first brought the Spencers prosperity. From July of '98 on, tens of thousands of feet scrunched over the gravel paths of Dianaville. The huge stable block was given a £2 million refit and is now a museum. A wistful legend now haunts the Oval Lake.

For Althorp, Charles Dickens might have said the preceding eleven months had been the worst and the best of times. Princess Diana died violently. The Earl suffered divorce and ongoing controversy. Yet the stately home is on the map as never before and its earning power as a tourist attraction seems cast in grey Weldon stone. Althorp needs the cash. Even with serious old money like that of seventeen Spencer generations, fortunes come and go. Not long before the late Earl Johnny Spencer gave his daughter to a prince in 1981, he had been forced to part with one million pounds in treasures from his private art collection. To cover death

duties and maintenance bills, a Van Dyck and other antiques were sold. He little dreamed that sixteen years later, a handful of Diana's old gowns would fetch more at auction than his precious Van Dyck.

The late "Johnny" Spencer inherited his Earldom in 1975. Embarrassed by their new titles of Ladies and Viscount, his children arrived at Althorp. Charles Spencer, now the ninth Earl, recalled his earliest vibes to author Andrew Morton: "it was like and old man's club with masses of clocks ticking away. For an impressionable child, it was a nightmarish place."

In time, Althorp became pile sweet pile and the children enjoyed their heritage. For the two-pound admission fee to Althorp in 1981, a knowledgeable 15-year-old Viscount Charles showed me and a tour party the exquisite Lely court portraits. Charles later recalled that his sister Diana used the stately entrance hall for ballet practice. Under threat of penury, Althorp was forced to commercialise in the 1980s. The siblings' new step mum, Raine Spencer, put in tea rooms, a gift shop and opened the cellars to wine-buyers. The Spencers poured tea for visitors and when Althorp's fame peaked through Diana's superstardom, they held formal nights where tourists paid £75 to dine with the Earl and his Countess. The children were contemptuous. In 1980, an American who employed Diana asked whether Althorp should be included in a proposed stately-home crawl. "I shouldn't bother," winced the young lady.

A cherubic Diana captured by her father, Johnny, who was a keen amateur photographer. (Facing page) Diana and younger brother Charles. After their parents' divorce, the seven year-old Diana became very protective of her brother. During the traumatic years of their early childhood when Charles used to cry during the night, Diana would go to his bed to console him.

Diana reading one of her step-grandmother, Barbara Cartland's, novels. After her death Dame Barbara Cartland recalled: "I was devoted to Princess Diana and we had a very close relationship. As a young girl she started reading (my) books which gave her a strong sense of romance and what she expected from the hero in her own life. Sadly, it did not work for her as it would have done in Barbara Cartland's books – although she did marry the handsome prince in a fairytale wedding. We all know that it did not work out and that is now history. When she was sixteen or seventeen, I said to her: 'You are so pretty now. You ought to be dancing with young men, like I was at your age.' I always called her the Princess of Love. I don't think she was terribly happy . . . I think she missed quite a lot in life, but she made up for it by giving so much love and people gave her love." (Facing page) A young Diana in a photograph that captures the beauty-to-come of the later Princess of Wales.

By now, of course, her brother faces the same financial realities as his father. In 1998, the young Earl wrote to me (and everyone who reserved a nine pound fifty pence ticket for his debut tourist season at Althorp). "I hope you will find your visit to Althorp reassures you that Diana is safely back home . . . where her mortal remains can be cared for, and where her memory lives on forever."

The new museum has its critics. But it displays Diana's relics tastefully and does not manipulate visitors' emotions. Her evening gowns and day outfits adorn faceless mannequins. The piped-in music is classical. Her childhood toys and Beatrix Potter animals could be the treasures of any little girl, especially the china bunnies with missing ears. There is no commentary. Items such as Diana's 1979 Christmas gift list speaks volumes for the young lady whose prince has not yet come: a sewing box from Aunt Lavinia; handkerchiefs from a Mrs Pearce; a five-pound voucher from a Mrs Fox.

"What we are doing here," said Charles Spencer, "is showing Diana as she was and what she achieved . . . also where she came from and the family she was part of." His shop, he said, would sell "a select range of goods inspired by Diana yet not cheapening her memory . . ." Indeed, not a single item in the packed gift shop bore his sister's image or name. While not actually commercialising Diana, almost every gift-shop item (including the purple carrier bags), proudly bore the name of

Diana **26** *an English rose*

1974: Diana with her Shetland pony "Souffle" and (facing page) at her mother's home in Scotland. Fishing at Balmoral during her engagement. Although Diana was raised as a country girl, later in life — perhaps because of the isolation and loneliness caused by her failing marriage — she craved the hustle and bustle of the big city.

Diana's grandmother Lady Ruth Fermoy who, along with the Queen Mother, encouraged the blossoming romance between Charles and Diana. At the time of Diana's parents' divorce, Lady Fermoy supported Earl Spencer rather than Diana's mother, Frances, during the battle for the custody of the children.

England's most commercial stately home, Althorp. Nostalgia aside, the Spencers have always been practical. It was the fifth Earl who bought the little temple now dedicated to Diana, for just three pounds in the 1880s. He had the timbers transported from Admiralty House in London (he was First Lord of the Admiralty) and reassembled in their present position. The revamped temple casts a classical reflection in a lake designed by 18th Century landscaping guru, Capability Brown. At its centre, the tiny island protecting Diana's remains was where she buried her favourite cat, Marmalade. Rising from the island is a sculpted urn, surmounted by a flame.

Traditionally, family grandees are interred in the Spencer vault of St Mary's Church in Great Brington. But Charles Spencer deemed this inappropriate for Diana. "Someone could get in (to the vault) and do something appalling," he explained. "Then I thought: it's got to be the (Althorp) park. She loved it here." It must be observed that to construct a hole deep and dry enough to bury the Princess on the low island – in the few days between death and funeral – was surely a daunting feat of engineering. Yet despite some scepticism that Diana actually lies here, Charles Spencer swears "on my life and on my children's lives, this is where Diana is buried."

To locals in Great Brington (population one hundred and seventy five), the youngest Spencer daughter was a well-liked but unromanticised personality. "It's hard to imagine her as the international figure she became," an eighty-six year-old church steward told me. "She was just a nice, quiet, country girl . . ."

The first Sir John Spencer bought the core of Althorp in 1508. Enlarged over the centuries, the house is now bigger than most of the Queen's homes and sits on 13,000 Spencer acres. Treasures inside reflect the fortunes of a family that has long farmed, climbed politically and passed on the DNA for ambitious marriages. Virtual sainthood also afflicted the clan before Diana. In the 19th century, a George Spencer converted to Catholicism and worked with the down-trodden. His followers are still petitioning Rome for his canonisation.

From her mother's side, Diana was related to eight American presidents. The Fermoy connection includes Diana's late grandmother Ruth, who was best friend and Woman of the Bedchamber to the Queen mother. George VI hunted with the seventh Earl, Jack Spencer, and encouraged little Princess Elizabeth to

play with his friend's son. In time, "Johnny" was equerry to both George VI and
Elizabeth II. Thirty years before Diana's first triumphant Commonwealth tour, her
father saw similar adulation for his lovely young Queen on antipodean shores.

Despite her uncommon ancestry, Prince Charles' would marry a commoner.
And from birth, she was beset with common woes. Early teachers and her siblings
saw her as insecure. In the words of her last nanny, Mary Clarke, Diana was "little
girl lost." She never recovered from her parents' divorce; never overcame the view
of herself as "the girl who was supposed to be a boy."

Diana would become the joy of her "darling daddy." Before his death in
1992, the eighth Earl marvelled: "Someone said to me that the two most famous
people in the world are the Pope and my daughter. I am so proud of Diana!" But at
her birth in 1961, he already had two daughters (Jane and Sarah) and a male heir
was badly needed. An earlier son had died in infancy and the Earl's marriage to
Frances Burke Roche was already on the rocks when – three years after Diana –

September 16, 1989. The marriage of Viscount Althorp, Diana's brother, to model Victoria Lockwood. The Eighteenth century-style wedding which took place at Great Brington near the Spencer family home of Althorp was beautifully planned. (Facing page, clockwise from top left) Prince Harry, with cousin Eleanor Fellowes, dressed in period costume copied from a portrait of a former Viscount Althorp by Joshua Reynolds. All the bridesmaids and pageboys were nieces and nephews of Viscount Althorp; Diana and William; Diana with her mother Mrs Frances Shand Kydd arriving at the church; Earl Spencer and wife Raine.

Diana was told of her father's death, on March 29, 1992, whilst holidaying in Lech, Austria, with Prince Charles and sons William and Harry. She was prepared to fly home alone, feeling that on Charles' part his immediate return would be only a gesture; but after the Queen's request that Charles be allowed to join her, Diana acquiesced. (Right) A grieving Diana on her return to England and (below) Diana carrying her father's ashes. (Facing page) Charles and Diana at the funeral on the Althorp Estate.

Charles came along. Park House, on the Queen's Sandringham Estate, should have been a heavenly place for the Spencer children to grow up. The ocean was just miles away. When the Windsors were in residence, Spencer children played with royal youngsters. Diana enjoyed a swimming pool, a tennis court and wide open spaces to play.

But by the age of seven, Diana thought her world was falling apart. To society, her parents were the perfect pair. Privately, they fought. A lifetime later, Diana told of the apocalyptic day she huddled on the stairs and her father loaded mummy's suitcases into a car. The Viscountess was driven away and eventually married Peter Shand Kydd. After much legal muck-raking, Johnny Spencer won custody of the children.

Sighed Diana of the following years: "Too many nannies. The whole thing was very unstable." She and her brother feared the dark and Charles sobbed at night. Sometimes Diana crawled into bed with him, more often she was frightened to leave her room. Daddy was kindly but detached. He bought the swimming pool, the beach buggy and heaped toys on them at Christmas. But Charles was seven before he was invited to share a dinner table with the Earl. "Charles said to me he hadn't realised how much the divorce had affected him until he got married," said Diana. "(It) helped me relate to anyone else who is upset in their family life . . . I understand it. Been there, done that."

In their first uniforms, Diana and Charles scrunched miserably off to Silfield school near Park House. Jean Lowe, then headmistress, recalls Diana as a skin-hungry pupil: "Viscount Althorp was of a generation that didn't kiss or cuddle . . . when Diana came and read to me she would lean against me . . . she wanted that physical touch." (Years later, Diana often declared her heartfelt doctrine that "children need hugs.")

Charles was academic. Diana was not. But she had an early talent for comforting and mothered her little brother. The Honourable Charles and Diana were the only children in their circle with divorced parents and never felt they belonged. Diana would burst into tears in class and pathetically, dedicated all her paintings "to mummy and daddy." She took great care not to show favouritism to either parent. On train rides home after a weekend with mummy, she composed herself not to seem too overjoyed to see daddy again. One endearing relic in the Althorp museum is a 1966 letter to "mummy and daddy" in Diana's childish scrawl. By the age of nine, "little girl lost" was certain of one thing: she told nanny Mary Clarke that when she married, it would be "for love alone. Otherwise it ends up in divorce."

Among her family and girlfriends, Diana was called "Duch", short for duchess. The name stuck until death. "Duch" certainly had her headstrong ways. Far from trying to cultivate the royal connection, "I used to kick and fight anyone who tried to make us go, (to Sandringham)" said Diana. "The atmosphere was always very strange . . . I didn't want to see *Chitty Chitty Bang Bang* for the third year running." She was not in awe of the Queen, who was simply a family friend and godmother to her little brother. But Diana was very conscious of royal

etiquette and scolded her nanny for forgetting a curtsy to Princess Alexandra.

Though meticulously tidy, "Duch" was not vain. She grew so quickly that she only ever had one smart dress that fitted and her hair, said Mary Clarke, "looked as if it could do with a good brush." She was more passionate about grooming her beloved guinea pig – Peanuts – one of a series of small animals she carted around in cages.

Howling in protest, Diana was packed off to West Heath boarding school at 13. She told Andrew Morton of her reputation for "always looking for trouble . . . I always won the swimming and diving cups . . . prizes for the best-kept guinea pig . . . but in the academic department, you might as well forget about that." A 1973 report card shows her best subject was religious knowledge. For Latin she scored a dismal thirty three per cent and a comment: "a poor memory greatly reduces her output." But she danced as one born for it. Her headmistress Ruth Rudge remembers: "Anyone who came down (to the school gym) before breakfast would see her leaping about in great swoops and whirls."

Though in the shadow of brilliant older sisters, Diana did well at the piano. But West Heath's tradition of community service brought out the best in its student. At a nearby mental hospital, she would crawl on the linoleum to make emotional contact with patients. Her magic with the disturbed people was instinctive, but hospital volunteer Muriel Stevens taught her to "stoop down so you always are on eye level . . . take hold of their hands."

Much later, on her maid's day off at Kensington Palace, Diana would scrub her own bath tub. Even at school, she was passionate for domesticity. Diana loved the kitchen staff and even won a prize for "helpfulness". With the same people-pleasing zeal at Althorp one Christmas, she rewrapped one of her own gifts and gave it to a grumpy staffer. The man cried from gratitude. In his famous eulogy, Charles Spencer summed Diana up as "a very insecure person at heart, almost childlike in her desire to do good . . . so she could release herself from deep feelings of unworthiness . . ." As a child and as a princess, Diana always sought watery places for her moods of introspection. In Scotland, she would ponder a loch; in London, the Serpentine and at Althorp, she mooched alone on the island where her unmarked grave now lies.

Alas, kindness and introspection did not win O-Levels. Said her piano teacher Penny Walker: "the staff knew she was struggling . . . she was distracted by the awful torment in her family at the time." At sixteen years old, Lady Diana left school with no formal qualifications. "I wasn't good at anything," she said. "I felt hopeless, a dropout." When she became a princess, even her maid had better exam results than she. In 1982 I heard her tell Tetbury children: "I was hopeless at maths and I never really understood the twenty four hour clock."

Swiss finishing school was her mother's idea. Far from improving her French, Diana dropped out early and flew home. Althorp was weathering more drama. Sarah Spencer, shrunken with anorexia, was dating Princes Charles. The Earl had remarried and the children hated his new Countess, Raine Dartmouth, daughter of novelist Barbara Cartland, was dainty, porcelain-skinned, and ambitious. She tore through the decaying family pile, selling treasures and gilding anything that stood still. Raine endured the "wicked stepmother lark" from the children. She pouted to Barbara Cartland: "whatever I do is wrong . . . they are so against me."

Mary Clarke summed up their resentment. "they had been surrounded by their father's love. They didn't want anyone else coming in." Dubbing the Countess "acid Raine," the children forgot that her measures kept Althorp solvent. She also saved the Earl's life, cajoling him back to health after a near fatal brain haemorrhage. The Countess later complained: "I could have saved my husband's life ten times over . . . and it wouldn't have changed anything in the children's attitude." She was banned from the family pew at the Wedding of the Century. But thanks to Raine, Diana could still cling to her "darling daddy" on that agonising walk up the aisle.

During the intervening years, the future Princess of Wales cleaned a friend's house for one pound an hour; did a cookery course and nannied for an American family. Her employer, Mary Robertson, learned of Diana's aristocracy only when a bank slip for Lady Diana Spencer surfaced. Diana brushed the American's astonishment aside. "The subject never came up again," said her boss. "It meant nothing to her."

Menial jobs merely supplemented an allowance from funds set up by her American great-grand mother. At eighteen years old, Diana used the fund to buy a fifty thousand pound Earls Court flat, (thanks to its royal connection, the same apartment would eighteen years later go on the market at four hundred and fifty thousand pounds). A teenage land lady, she wrote "chief chic" on her bed room door and sub-let to chums. Within a year, the fame of her home at Coleherne Court would almost eclipse that of Althorp.

Diana's farewell to her beloved father – the note accompanying her wreath for his funeral.

I'm terrified of making a promise and then, perhaps, living to regret it

Prince Charles, 1980

As a young mother, the Queen wanted Prince Charles to have a "normal" childhood. Sadly, she had little experience on which to base such an ideal. As the duties of heiress presumptive and soon of monarch took most of her time, a normal mother-and-son-bond was unlikely. Sailor Prince Philip was often at sea and the Queen usually saw her son for about thirty minutes after breakfast and for a little longer at bedtime. Even when the parents were together, duty took them on overseas trips that seemed cruelly long for everyone involved. They were rarely around to encourage his skills. So it was with nannies and servants that Charles developed. When Charles blew out the candles on his fifth birthday – in London – Prince Philip and the Queen stayed at Sandringham, preparing for a Commonwealth tour that would take them away for six months. In this manner, the boy learned what he did not want for his own sons; a generation later, he and his wife would take their infant William to Australia. The Queen may have yearned for a more hands-on

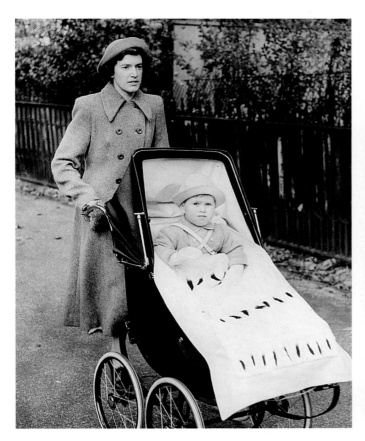

Toddler Charles at Windsor Castle with his mother, still Princess Elizabeth at the time, and (top, left) taking a breath of fresh air on his second birthday with nanny Mabel Anderson pushing the royal pram. (Left) The House of Windsor gathers in Buckingham Palace after the christening of the future King Charles III. (Left to right, standing) Lady Brabourne, the proud father Prince Philip, grandfather King George VI, the Honourable David Bowes-Lyon (the Queen Mother's brother), the Earl of Athlone, Princess Margaret. (Seated) The Marchioness of Milford Haven and Charles' great-grandmother Queen Mary on either side of the mother and baby.

(Facing page) Ever the gentleman even at the tender age of four in 1952, Charles leads the way for little sister Princess Anne.

Teenager Charles (above) with the two men who had the greatest influence on his formative years — father Philip and "Uncle Dickie", Earl Mountbatten. It was Mountbatten's advice for Charles to "sow his wild oats" before marriage — and it was Prince Philip who finally read the riot act to his son about providing an "heir and spare" that led to his marriage to Diana.

(Left) April 1962, Charles' first day at Gordonstoun, the school in Morayshire father Philip had attended before the war. But Charles did not share his father's enthusiasm for the spartan discipline that was the order of the day in the school on the shores of the Moray Firth. Many years later, he was to confess he had hated his time there. (Facing page, top) Charles relaxing in his room at Cambridge just prior to his investiture as Prince of Wales in 1969.

(Bottom, left) Happier moments with little brothers Andrew and Edward and (right) a stroll in the countryside with sister Anne and their father.

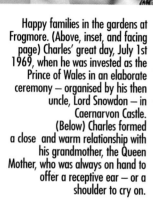

Happy families in the gardens at Frogmore. (Above, inset, and facing page) Charles' great day, July 1st 1969, when he was invested as the Prince of Wales in an elaborate ceremony – organised by his then uncle, Lord Snowdon – in Caernarvon Castle. (Below) Charles formed a close and warm relationship with his grandmother, the Queen Mother, who was always on hand to offer a receptive ear – or a shoulder to cry on.

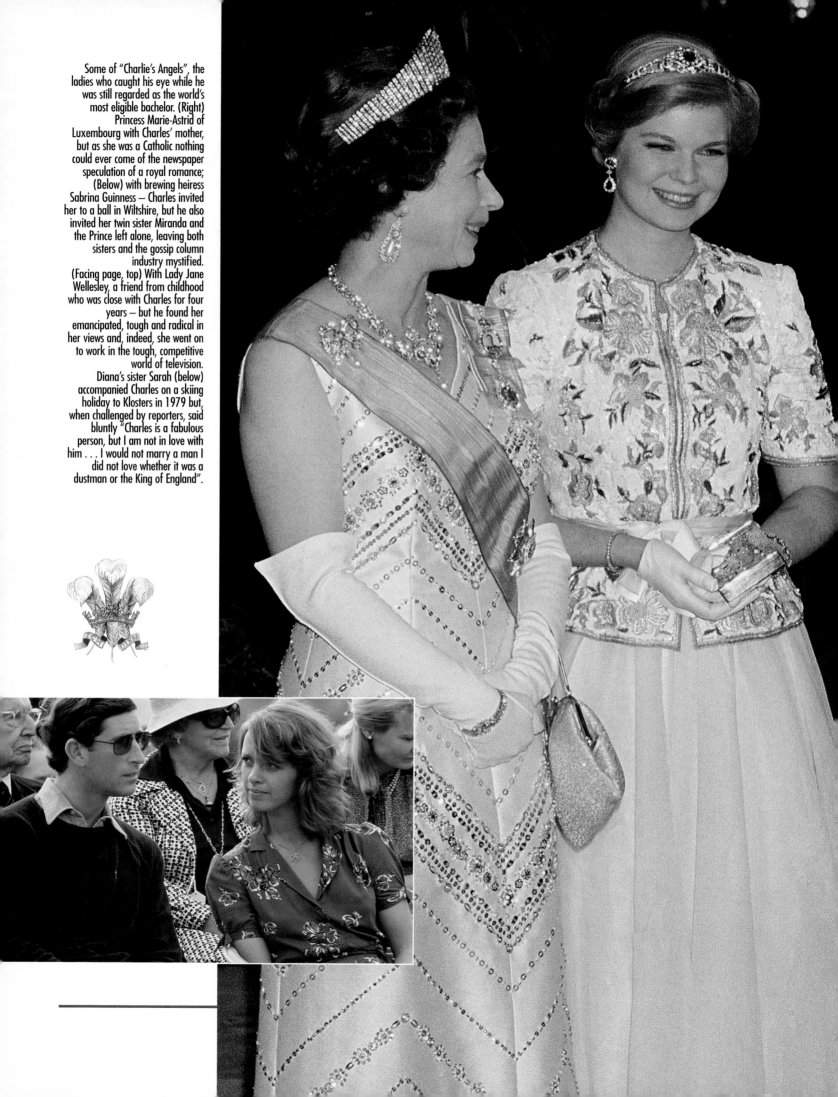

Some of "Charlie's Angels", the ladies who caught his eye while he was still regarded as the world's most eligible bachelor. (Right) Princess Marie-Astrid of Luxembourg with Charles' mother, but as she was a Catholic nothing could ever come of the newspaper speculation of a royal romance; (Below) with brewing heiress Sabrina Guinness — Charles invited her to a ball in Wiltshire, but he also invited her twin sister Miranda and the Prince left alone, leaving both sisters and the gossip column industry mystified.

(Facing page, top) With Lady Jane Wellesley, a friend from childhood who was close with Charles for four years — but he found her emancipated, tough and radical in her views and, indeed, she went on to work in the tough, competitive world of television.

Diana's sister Sarah (below) accompanied Charles on a skiing holiday to Klosters in 1979 but, when challenged by reporters, said bluntly "Charles is a fabulous person, but I am not in love with him . . . I would not marry a man I did not love whether it was a dustman or the King of England".

Diana **47** *an English rose*

motherhood, but duty was paramount and she deferred to her husband in family matters. Prince Philip had spartan ideals about child-rearing. They suited Princess Anne's boisterous confidence, but her brother was a bad fit for his father's stereotype of a steely future king. Charles did not know the huggy, hand-holding reinforcement that Princes William and Harry would get from both parents. "I want him (Charles) to be a man's man," said Prince Philip, giving him cricket bats instead of teddy bears. For cuddles, Charles went to his nanny. Or he climbed into his doting grandmother's lap. The Queen Mother was lavish with affection and their intimacy grew stronger than Charles' bond with any other family member.

At four years old he was awed by public emotion for his newly-crowned mother. It was no longer possible to believe he was the same as "normal" children. Created Prince of Wales at the age of ten, Charles accepted what he called the "awful truth" of a destiny from which he had no escape, and which would irresistibly shape every decision he made.

Charles was fond of saying "I am just an ordinary person in an extraordinary position." But as he reached adulthood, his experiences became more extraordinary. He was proclaimed an Indian chief in Canada, he commanded his own Naval ship, he piloted and parachuted out of jet planes, he dove beneath polar ice, wind-sailed and played polo like a demon. Finding a wife promised to be a feat of even greater daring. Though he was called the "most eligible bachelor on earth" Charles could not imagine anyone he might hope to marry who would actually want the life sentence – of discipline, duty, publicity – and the institution which came with him.

His surrogate grandfather, Lord Mountbatten, became a mentor in the quest. For somewhere to entertain lady friends, he loaned Charles his country seat,

The paths of Prince Charles and Camilla Parker Bowles crossed in 1972 when legend has it she introduced herself by reminding Charles that his great-great-grandfather Edward VII had been the lover of her great-great-grandmother, Alice Keppel. (Above) A night on the town with Camilla and her future husband Andrew Parker Bowles. The friendship continued during the Parker Bowles' marriage and re-emerged into the full glare of publicity when Charles admitted on television that he had committed adultery after the "irretrievable breakdown" of his marriage with Diana. The mature, divorced Camilla (facing page) was then cast in the role of the Scarlet Woman who had been a major factor in the Wales' marriage breakdown.

Broadlands. He gave this advice: "A man should sew his wild oats and have as many affairs as he can before settling down. But for a wife, he should choose a suitable and sweet-charactered girl before she meets anyone else she might fall for." If this sounds uncannily like Diana Spencer, the Earl had dynastic visions and was promoting his grand-daughter, Amanda Knatchbull, as a royal bride.

In the meantime, Lady Jane Wellesley (a descendant of Waterloo's Lord Wellington), declined his suit. Davina Sheffield had "a past" and – to Charles' great misery – was ruled out by Mountbatten. Lady Sarah Spencer made the error of telling a reporter she did not love her royal beau. In his travels with the Navy, Charles was everywhere besieged by ambitious girls and their mothers and had plenty of opportunity to follow Mountbatten's wild-oats advice.

The press portrayed Charles as a playboy and dubbed his girlfriends "Charlie's Angels." In flights of fantasy, they also had Charles enamoured of Princess Marie-Astrid of Luxembourg and Princess Caroline of Monaco. But the Prince took his quest for a Princess of Wales and future Queen consort very seriously. She would have to make terrific sacrifices. "A woman not only marries a man," he pondered. "She marries into a way of life . . . she's got to have some knowledge of it . . . or she wouldn't have a clue about whether she's going to like it. And if she didn't have a clue, it would be risky for her, wouldn't it?"

One of the young women Charles invited to Broadlands was Camilla Shand, who was horsy, attractive and exactly his type. She became a confidante; an outlet for his loneliness. But he dilly-dallied about proposing and gave her time to marry Andrew Parker-Bowles. Women flitted in and out of his life until, by 1979, Charles found himself at the age of thirty. Just when his courtship of Mountbatten's grand-daughter Amanda looked extremely promising, Charles' mentor was assassinated by the IRA. The young couple would have obeyed Mountbatten's every wish but without his patronage, the arranged "romance" died from mutual apathy. His next flame, Anna Wallace, was too free-spirited for her conservative suitor. More shockingly, she found Scotland a bore.

Charles with another of his long-term female friends, Dale Tryon, whom he called "Kanga". The Australian-born "Kanga" died in 1997 after a long illness, but for many years had been regarded as an important member of the Prince's inner circle of friends. The Queen and Queen Mother thoroughly approved of Diana and Lady Tryon was one of the two married women among the Prince's friends who were all for the marriage – the other was Camilla Parker-Bowles.

By 1980, Charles was exasperated that speculation on his love life deflected attention from any sensible role he tried to find for himself. "The media will simply not take me seriously until I do get married and apparently become responsible," he said. It had been a long search and, by now, to find a female who fitted Mountbatten's antiquated ideal, Charles would have to peer into cradles.

But by February of 1981, he had located the girl, proposed and been accepted. She chose a ring so large that even she found it impractical. "I scratched my nose with it," she confessed at a garden party. "It's so big. The ring, that is." The 19-year-old Lady Diana Spencer was installed in Buckingham Palace and with relief that was shared by the nation, The Prince of Wales took off to tour the Antipodes.

I told her she must marry the man she loves

Earl Spencer, 1981

The young lady was left to pine in London. But for his final bachelor tour, Charles was in splendid form. Snowdon's gorgeous portraits of the fiancee – a wide-eyed ingenue with frilly blouse and rosebud – were wowing the planet. Charles seemed the luckiest man on earth. He even said so at every tour appearance: "I'm amazed that she's been brave enough to take me on," he told New Zealanders and Australians. Happiness brought out the clown in him. In New Zealand, I had to leap to safety after he had commandeered a child's bicycle and was swerving drunkenly through a walkabout. He laughed and posed when photographers set-up five "Lady Di look-alikes" (complete with frilly blouses) to corral him. The chortles continued in a ritual where Auckland sailors gave him a massive ball and chain. For the last time ever, Charles loved being the sole focus of attention.

No one took the ball and chain seriously. But the Prince of Wales had been carefully stalked and snared by Diana the Huntress. His valet, Steven Barry, later told me: "She went after the Prince with one thing in mind. She wanted him – and she got him!" Diana's aim was clear to everyone; even Charles spoke of realising "what was going on in my mind and (in) hers in particular."

Still, all is fair in love. And Diana was besotted. Spencers had been mingling with kings for five hundred years, so marrying into royalty had always been a reasonable option. Vivacious elder sister Sarah first brought Charles tantalisingly close to Diana. But even before the notion of being Princess of Wales captivated her, Diana had known serious boyfriends were out. "I knew I had to keep myself tidy for what lay ahead," she said. Her big break was a 1979 vacation with her sister

At the age of 19 Diana could have simply enjoyed the life of a Sloane Ranger, but she had different priorities and showed her caring instinct by choosing to be a nanny. Prior to her marriage she shared her flat in Kensington with two girl friends. The young Diana usually kept her cool when being chased by photographers (right) after the word was out that she was "Charlie's latest Angel".
(Facing page) September 1980. Lady Diana, thinking the photographers would relent, agreed to let them take some pictures at her place of work, the Young England Kindergarten at Pimlico, London. Those pictures made the newspaper front pages — she was not wearing a petticoat and the sunlight gave the nation a good shot of the future Princess of Wales' fabulous legs.

Jane, who had married the courtier Robert Fellowes. In summer, the Fellowes used a house in the Balmoral estate. Rambling among the heather, it was easy for Diana to encounter and charm Prince Charles. Her warmth was appealing. After Lord Mountbatten's death, Diana's innocent condolences touched him as more stilted approaches could not. Colleagues at the Young England Kindergarten remember Diana as the teenager who could always find the unhappy child in a group. This time, Charles was her needy one. She told him: "You looked so sad when you walked up the aisle (at his uncle's funeral). My heart bled for you . . . you're lonely – you should be with somebody to look after you." The Prince at once was smitten.

When she returned to Balmoral in autumn, Diana had a royal suitor. She and Prince Charles shared walks, barbecues and long hours fishing in the River Dee. She found everything about Balmoral "magical," because she was in love. Not just with Charles, but with the whole fantasy of being his wife and looking after him forever. Back in London, she acted nonchalantly with the woman for whom she nannied. "Do you think there's any chance of a romance developing?" asked Mary Robertson. "Not really," sighed Diana. "After all he's 31 and I'm only 19. He'd never look at me seriously . . ."

Days before the wedding, the fashion-conscious Diana in a lilac and yellow striped suit with feather hat watching polo at Windsor A sign of what was to come – a photographer is behind her. (Facing page) May 1981. Her first visit to Tetbury, the village nearest her future husband's country home, Highgrove. The months before the wedding Diana was thrust into the world of royal activities and somehow she seemed to cope and people fell in love with the young kindergarten assistant.

She soon got a preview of how the rest of her "forever" would be. Newsmen spotted her at Balmoral and – blimey! Hold the front page! – the hunt was on for Charlie's latest angel. As Princess Anne was to observe, rather drily, some time later: "(Diana) obviously filled a void in the media's life which I had not filled . . ." As quickly as Charles, Fleet Street fell in love. But while the Prince still nursed doubts, the press had already chosen Diana for Princess of Wales. She was Protestant, a virgin at 19 years old and, most importantly, an asset to newspaper sales. They could overlook two sets of twice-married parents. Goodness knows, even the Queen's sister was a divorcee.

Round-the-clock observation at Coleherne Court began. There was no

1981, March. Lady Diana at Romsey, Hampshire, where she would later start her honeymoon at Earl Mountbatten's home, Broadlands.
On Ladies Day at Ascot just before her wedding (right) Diana chose a pale apricot suit, an outfit she also wore during her honeymoon.
(Facing page) The couple pose at Balmoral with a backdrop of the beautiful Scottish Highlands.

On March 9, 1981, the fiancée of the future King stunned everybody with this very low-cut black dress, when she attended a poetry and musical recital at Goldsmith's Hall. Princess Grace of Monaco was there, too, and chatted with the shy Diana (below, inset). Diana later said that to wear black at that age made her feel glamorous and grown-up. However, the Royal Family did not appreciate her gesture — they wear black strictly for funerals. (Facing page) July 1981. Four days before the wedding at the Guards Polo Club. Diana looks pensive and under stress as thousands of people turned up to see the future Princess of Wales.

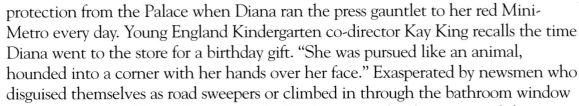

protection from the Palace when Diana ran the press gauntlet to her red Mini-Metro every day. Young England Kindergarten co-director Kay King recalls the time Diana went to the store for a birthday gift. "She was pursued like an animal, hounded into a corner with her hands over her face." Exasperated by newsmen who disguised themselves as road sweepers or climbed in through the bathroom window and by traffic jams in the Pimlico street, her bosses agreed that Diana should face the cameras and pose just once. Those famous shots of her see-through skirt devastated Diana. She never trusted her modesty to cameramen again. Years later in Italy, she was told her dresses were too long and dowdy. "I like to bend down to talk to children," she explained "and I don't want photographers to see anything they shouldn't."

At a polo match at Tidworth where Charles was competing, Diana was overcome by emotion and tears came to her eyes (above & facing page). She coped better with the photographers and the crowds immediately after the engagement announcement than in the months before the wedding. She then realised that the interest in her was not going to lessen and the pressure was becoming too much for her. As she said later, no help was forthcoming from the Palace. She realised that she had to "swim or sink" without help or advice.

At Coleherne Court, the press recorded giggles, blushes but never a word from her. She had perfected a technique of saying nothing but hinting volumes with a twinkling eye and a smirk. The look hinted – as she would famously predict shortly before her death – "you're all in for a surprise." She had been schooled by her sister that a loose tongue would scuttle all patient manoeuvering.

If Diana's ambiguous situation made life impossible, the Queen saw it all as a test, reasoning: "Well, she is going to have to get used to this kind of thing . . ." But as more visits to Scotland and more rambling in the Cotswolds ensued, the royal paramour would still not commit. He even showed Diana to his new home at Tetbury, asking for advice with interior decor. In the absence of any proposal, she thought his questions "most improper". Exasperated, she confided in American Mary Robertson: "I will simply die if this doesn't work out, I won't be able to show my face."

The tom-tom of rumour grew so intolerable in town that Northamptonshire was the only place Diana could find peace. Her friend and confidante, Lady Elsa Bowker, telephoned Althorp and asked after the beleaguered young woman. Diana was walking alone in the grounds. "She's crying because Charles is not proposing," stepmother Raine told Lady Bowker. At last, Prince Philip interrupted the procrastination. The fatherly ultimatum was that Charles should either propose or end the affair before Diana's reputation was ruined.

No candles. No soft guitars. But the question Diana craved came over dinner at Windsor Castle. The couple ate poached salmon and drank mineral water. Typically, the suitor used hypothetical terms: "If I were to ask, what do you think you might answer?" he began. "Yes", was her reply. "It wasn't a difficult question," Diana recalled. "It was what I wanted."

All gallantry, Charles called Earl Spencer and asked "Can I marry your daughter, sir?" Diana's wishes were abundantly clear to her father. "She has no qualms about the responsibility," said the Earl. "She has no qualms about anything . . . I told her she must marry the man she loves and she said : 'that's what I'm

doing'." Nevertheless, Diana was quickly bundled off to Australia, where she skulked at the Shand Kydd's farm and pondered her future.

The betrothal was announced on February 24, 1981. Diana moved into Buckingham Palace. Her fiance completed his triumphant tour Down Under. Enthralled by pageantry and the gothic ideal of the virgin bride, Charles planned a wedding that he thought the Commonwealth wanted. "I can't wait for the whole thing," he enthused. "I want everyone to come out having had a marvellous musical and emotional experience." Preoccupied with fanfares and arias, he overlooked nurturing a partnership the Commonwealth deserved. Diana had arrived at the Palace with two suitcases of clothes and nearly twenty years of emotional baggage.

Those kisses and cuddles Barbara Cartland's novels had taught her to associate with high romance were absent during the betrothal. Royal aide Michael Colborne helped Diana find her feet at the Palace. "It must have been very daunting," he said later. "Diana was a vulnerable 19 year old. Charles was 32 but seemed almost middle-aged . . . she asked me what the future held. I explained she'd never be on her own again." Colborne had high hopes for the marriage. "I firmly believe he loved her and wanted to spend the rest of his days with her . . . there was an obvious tenderness and affection. But it was clear Diana loved Charles even more than he loved her."

The couple appeared at garden parties, race meetings and film premieres. Headlines gushed and the world was convinced of their happiness. Diana thought they would grow closer in the months before the wedding. "I am on a cloud," she wrote to her former employer Mary Robertson. But it was not always cloud nine. In fact, Diana and Charles had little private time together. Isolated, insecure and getting suspicious of the omnipresent Camilla Parker-Bowles, Diana took to a binge-and-purge eating habit. It was the start of the bulimia that haunted the entire marriage. Palace staff wondered how she could eat like a rugby player and shrink daily. In five months, she dropped three dress sizes. This was blithely dismissed in a letter to Mary Robertson: "Every fitting of my wedding dress has to be taken in – I'm sure it has a lot to do with nervous energy and there is PLENTY of that!" Said Michael Colborne: "As the wedding drew closer she became very apprehensive. She was naive, out of her depth and lost."

All Britain was a flurry of pre-wedding excitement when, the Sunday before "Di-Day," I watched Diana's face crumple into tears. She ran blindly from the Tidworth polo game and one heartless Fleet Streeter joked : "She probably wants to call the whole thing off!" Too cruel, I thought. All brides get hysterical. Besides, Diana Spencer's face was on tea towels from here to Alice Springs.

Ironically, it had been former nanny Mary Clarke who phoned the Palace and reminded Diana of her childhood vow to marry only for love. "You are marrying the one person," said the nanny, "from whom it would be impossible to be divorced."

THE ROYAL DESCENT OF THE PRINCE OF WALES

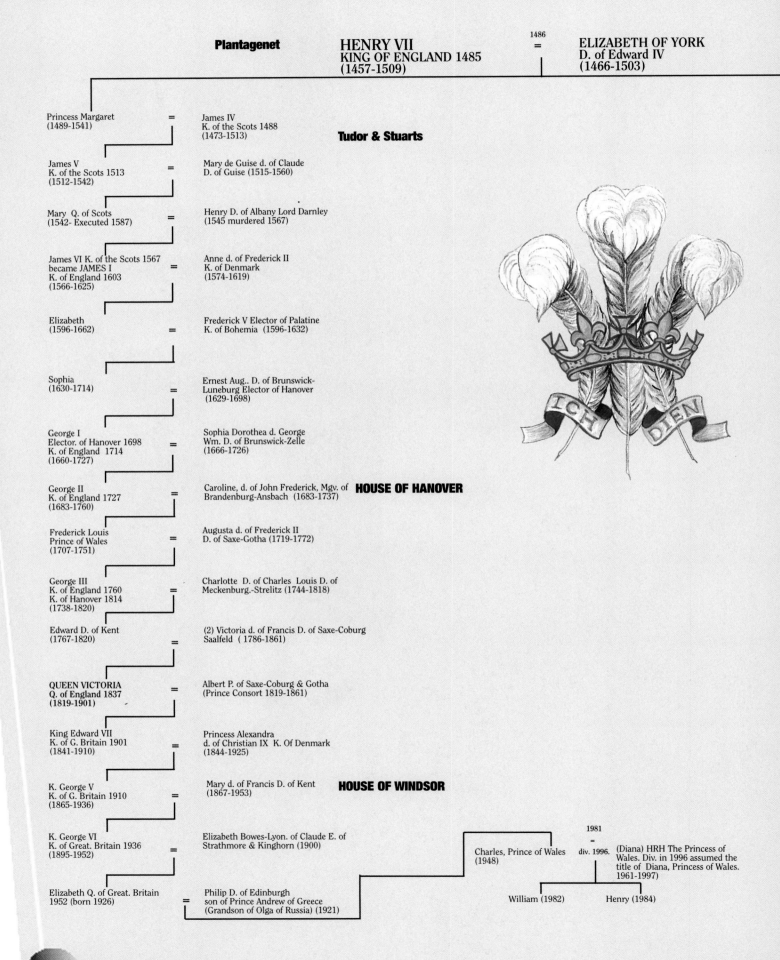

Plantagenet

HENRY VII
KING OF ENGLAND 1485
(1457-1509)

1486
=

ELIZABETH OF YORK
D. of Edward IV
(1466-1503)

Princess Margaret
(1489-1541)
=
James IV
K. of the Scots 1488
(1473-1513)

Tudor & Stuarts

James V
K. of the Scots 1513
(1512-1542)
=
Mary de Guise d. of Claude
D. of Guise (1515-1560)

Mary Q. of Scots
(1542- Executed 1587)
=
Henry D. of Albany Lord Darnley
(1545 murdered 1567)

James VI K. of the Scots 1567
became JAMES I
K. of England 1603
(1566-1625)
=
Anne d. of Frederick II
K. of Denmark
(1574-1619)

Elizabeth
(1596-1662)
=
Frederick V Elector of Palatine
K. of Bohemia (1596-1632)

Sophia
(1630-1714)
=
Ernest Aug.. D. of Brunswick-
Luneburg Elector of Hanover
(1629-1698)

George I
Elector. of Hanover 1698
K. of England 1714
(1660-1727)
=
Sophia Dorothea d. George
Wm. D. of Brunswick-Zelle
(1666-1726)

George II
K. of England 1727
(1683-1760)
=
Caroline, d. of John Frederick, Mgv. of
Brandenburg-Ansbach (1683-1737) **HOUSE OF HANOVER**

Frederick Louis
Prince of Wales
(1707-1751)
=
Augusta d. of Frederick II
D. of Saxe-Gotha (1719-1772)

George III
K. of England 1760
K. of Hanover 1814
(1738-1820)
=
Charlotte D. of Charles Louis D. of
Meckenburg.-Strelitz (1744-1818)

Edward D. of Kent
(1767-1820)
=
(2) Victoria d. of Francis D. of Saxe-Coburg
Saalfeld (1786-1861)

QUEEN VICTORIA
Q. of England 1837
(1819-1901)
=
Albert P. of Saxe-Coburg & Gotha
(Prince Consort 1819-1861)

King Edward VII
K. of G. Britain 1901
(1841-1910)
=
Princess Alexandra
d. of Christian IX K. Of Denmark
(1844-1925)

K. George V
K. of G. Britain 1910
(1865-1936)
=
Mary d. of Francis D. of Kent
(1867-1953) **HOUSE OF WINDSOR**

K. George VI
K. of Great. Britain 1936
(1895-1952)
=
Elizabeth Bowes-Lyon. of Claude E. of
Strathmore & Kinghorn (1900)

1981
=
div. 1996.

Charles, Prince of Wales
(1948)

(Diana) HRH The Princess of
Wales. Div. in 1996 assumed the
title of Diana, Princess of Wales.
1961-1997)

Elizabeth Q. of Great. Britain
1952 (born 1926)
=
Philip D. of Edinburgh
son of Prince Andrew of Greece
(Grandson of Olga of Russia) (1921)

William (1982)

Henry (1984)

& DIANA, PRINCESS OF WALES, FROM HENRY VII

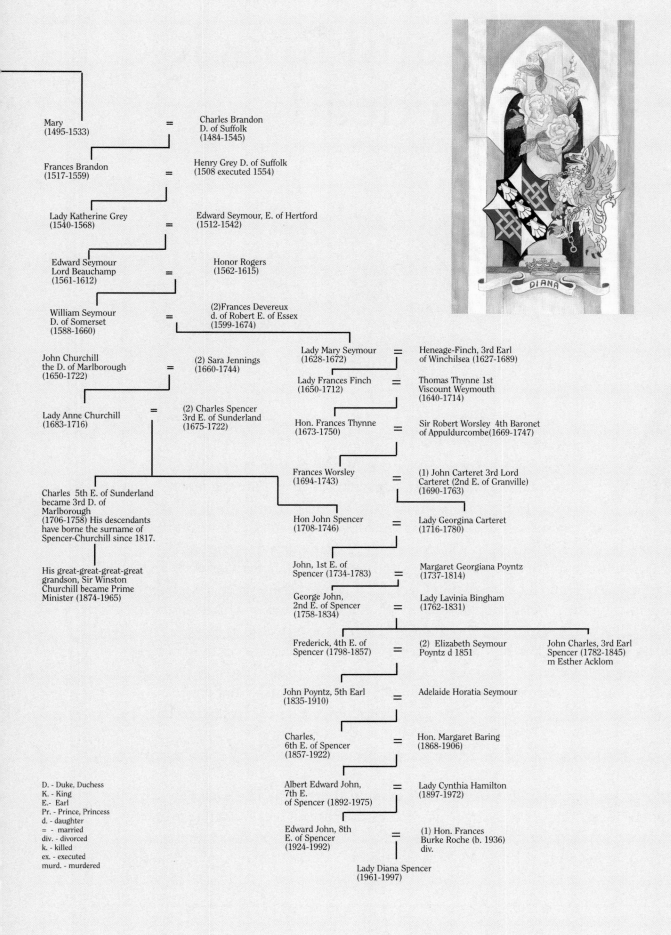

Mary
(1495-1533)
= Charles Brandon
D. of Suffolk
(1484-1545)

Frances Brandon
(1517-1559)
= Henry Grey D. of Suffolk
(1508 executed 1554)

Lady Katherine Grey
(1540-1568)
= Edward Seymour, E. of Hertford
(1512-1542)

Edward Seymour
Lord Beauchamp
(1561-1612)
= Honor Rogers
(1562-1615)

William Seymour
D. of Somerset
(1588-1660)
= (2)Frances Devereux
d. of Robert E. of Essex
(1599-1674)

Lady Mary Seymour
(1628-1672)
= Heneage-Finch, 3rd Earl
of Winchilsea (1627-1689)

John Churchill
the D. of Marlborough
(1650-1722)
= (2) Sara Jennings
(1660-1744)

Lady Frances Finch
(1650-1712)
= Thomas Thynne 1st
Viscount Weymouth
(1640-1714)

Lady Anne Churchill
(1683-1716)
= (2) Charles Spencer
3rd E. of Sunderland
(1675-1722)

Hon. Frances Thynne
(1673-1750)
= Sir Robert Worsley 4th Baronet
of Appuldurcombe(1669-1747)

Frances Worsley
(1694-1743)
= (1) John Carteret 3rd Lord
Carteret (2nd E. of Granville)
(1690-1763)

Charles 5th E. of Sunderland
became 3rd D. of
Marlborough
(1706-1758) His descendants
have borne the surname of
Spencer-Churchill since 1817.

Hon John Spencer
(1708-1746)
= Lady Georgina Carteret
(1716-1780)

His great-great-great-great
grandson, Sir Winston
Churchill became Prime
Minister (1874-1965)

John, 1st E. of
Spencer (1734-1783)
= Margaret Georgiana Poyntz
(1737-1814)

George John,
2nd E. of Spencer
(1758-1834)
= Lady Lavinia Bingham
(1762-1831)

Frederick, 4th E. of
Spencer (1798-1857)
= (2) Elizabeth Seymour
Poyntz d 1851

John Charles, 3rd Earl
Spencer (1782-1845)
m Esther Acklom

John Poyntz, 5th Earl
(1835-1910)
= Adelaide Horatia Seymour

Charles,
6th E. of Spencer
(1857-1922)
= Hon. Margaret Baring
(1868-1906)

D. - Duke, Duchess
K. - King
E.- Earl
Pr. - Prince, Princess
d. - daughter
= - married
div. - divorced
k. - killed
ex. - executed
murd. - murdered

Albert Edward John,
7th E.
of Spencer (1892-1975)
= Lady Cynthia Hamilton
(1897-1972)

Edward John, 8th
E. of Spencer
(1924-1992)
= (1) Hon. Frances
Burke Roche (b. 1936)
div.

Lady Diana Spencer
(1961-1997)

Just look 'em in the eye and knock 'em dead

Prince Charles to Diana at St Paul's Cathedral

s I took my £30 press seat for the "Wedding of the Century" I considered the day a yardstick event of my life. Like the moon landing. But cruel fate would make a later procession – in which Diana was again central – even more epoch-making. Still, I will never forget that sunny day in June 1981. London was a rainbow of bunting. Heart-stopping was Diana's slow walk up the aisle. Endearing was the bride who muffed her vows and almost married "Philip Charles Arthur George". It seemed there would be a happy ending for what the Archbishop of Canterbury called "the stuff of which fairy tales are made." About 750 million people watched as, for the first time in living memory, a Prince and Princess of Wales wed. Charles Spencer saw his mothering sister Diana transformed: "It was the first time in my life I ever thought of Diana as beautiful," he told Andrew Morton. "She really did look stunning that day . . . although she was slightly pale." In the royal pew, the Queen Mother dabbed her eyes.

"You look lovely," Prince Charles whispered as they knelt. "Lovely for you," replied Diana.

It was a wonder Diana looked so heavenly. Billeted on The Mall side of Clarence House, Diana was assailed all night by the crowd's revelry and had barely slept. Her bulimia was in full force. She had raided the Queen Mother's kitchen, eaten everything and made herself "sick as a parrot". Concerned next morning that

Diana **69** *an English rose*

altar microphones might pick up the rumbling of her stomach, she for once ate breakfast. In her bath tub, she contemplated what she would later call "the most emotionally confusing day of my life". Her sisters had laughed at her qualms the day before: "your face is on the tea towels, Duch, so it's too late to chicken out now." Indeed, the wedding presents heaped like an Aladdin's trove at Buckingham Palace would have been a political nightmare to return. From Saudi Arabia alone came £75,000 worth of diamonds and sapphires. "Gosh, I'm becoming a very rich lady," she had exclaimed.

Resolutely on her wedding morning, Diana turned on the television, watched children waving flags and marvelled that the hysteria gripping the world was about her. She told her make-up artist Barbara Daly "This is an amazingly big fuss for the wedding of one girl." Charles was jolted awake by a hubbub he called "indescribable." From dawn, when The Mall's great gypsy camp had found its singing voice, Buckingham Palace had been under vocal siege. Royal relatives who packed the Palace had been lullabied the previous night and "Rule Britannia" was too much for Charles. "I found myself standing in the window with tears pouring down my face," he said.

By seven a.m., Elizabeth Emanuel was already ironing forty four yards of ivory silk. Superstitiously, the young couturier did not sew her last stitch until the gown and its owner wafted off to St Paul's. During six months of secret work at the Bond Street salon, she had code-named her client "Deborah Smythson-Wells". The dimensions of the bodice had been a work-in-progress for weeks; her client's waist had been twenty nine inches at the first fitting. Now it was twenty three inches and still shrinking. Tabloid headlines the day before had hollered: "We love you Di, but don't get any thinner!"

The new Princess of Wales' mother leaving the Cathedral, after the marriage, with the Duke of Edinburgh.
(Below) The marriage was performed by the Archbishop of Canterbury, Dr Robert Runcie, using the words of the 1594 prayer book, — although the bride did not promise to obey.
(Facing page) The full glory and spectacle of the interior of St Paul's during the wedding ceremony.

The Prince and his new Princess of Wales walking past members of the Royal Family— (left to right) a smiling Queen, Prince Philip, Queen Mother and Prince Andrew. (Behind) Princess Anne, Captain Mark Phillips, Princess Margaret and their son Viscount Linley.
(Left) The bride and groom travel through London's streets back to Buckingham Palace after the marriage ceremony.
(Facing page) The ceremony has ended, Prince Charles and Diana walk down the nave of St Paul's, smiling to the guests, and followed by the bridesmaids and pages.

The crowds' first sight of the newlyweds (facing page) as they emerged from St Paul's to walk down the Cathedral steps to their waiting carriage. (Above). The return trip to Buckingham Palace was through streets bedecked with flowers and banners (left).

July 29, 1981. Dawn promised a beautiful bright day for the wedding of Charles and Diana. The streets between Buckingham Palace and St Paul's Cathedral were swarming with people, some had bedded down on pavements so as not to miss the view of this very special wedding. Flowers and banners appeared all over London, and among the display of wedding presents sent by ordinary members of the public was this sweet collection (above, inset) from children from all parts of Britain.

By 9.30am over 2,000 guests had taken their place in St Paul's Cathedral, among them over 160 foreign presidents, prime ministers and their wives, and monarchs from all over Europe, Africa and the Middle East. The culmination of a memorable day came when the newlyweds appeared (main picture) on the balcony of Buckingham Palace to be cheered by the gigantic crowds gathered there.

The official photograph recording the marriage. (Left to right, front row) Edward Van Cutsem, Clementine Hambro, Catherine Cameron, Sara Jane Gasalee and Lord Nicholas Windsor. (Middle row, left to right) Princess Anne, Princess Margaret, the Queen Mother, the Queen, India Hicks, Lady Sarah Armstrong-Jones, Mrs Shand Kydd, Earl Spencer, Lady Sarah McCorquodale and Neil McCorquodale. (Back row, left to right) Captain Mark Phillips, Prince Andrew, Viscount Linley, the Duke of Edinburgh, Prince Edward, the bride and groom, Ruth, Lady Fermoy, Lady Jane Fellowes, Viscount Althorp and Robert Fellowes.

Diana **81** *an English rose*

"Almighty God, the Father of our Lord Jesus Christ, pour upon you the riches of His Grace, sanctify you and bless you, that you may please Him both in body and soul, and live together in holy love unto your lives' end." The words with which the Archbishop blessed the couple (facing page) and ended the ceremony.

"Marriage is a much more important business than just falling in love . . . essentially you must be good friends and love, I'm sure, will grow out of that friendship and become deeper and deeper." (Prince Charles, in an interview in 1975 for *Woman's Own*)

"Next to Prince Charles, I can't go wrong. He is there with me." (Lady Diana Spencer in 1981 in an interview for BBC Television)

Her hairdresser, Kevin Shanley, stuck her hair in heated rollers but was dismayed when Diana sabotaged her own coiffure. "She had pulled the rollers out so she could talk to Prince Charles on the phone," he told me. India Hicks, one of the bridesmaids, watched the preparations. "The television was on and Diana was saying 'shoo, shoo' to anyone who got in her way. The 'just one cornetto' (ice-cream) ad came on TV and Diana started singing it, then we all joined in. Despite her nerves, Diana retained her sense of fun." The bride later gave each of her attendants a rose from her bouquet and a piece of silk from *The Dress*.

For the mood of the day, Diana's bouffant wedding crinoline was perfect. David and Elizabeth Emanuel were the hottest designers on the neo-romanticist scene. Says David: "She was such a romantic figure and we told her we would make her a fairy tale dress." They and their client scoured pictures of previous royal wedding dresses and Diana wanted to outdo them all. "We found out which dress had the longest train," said Elizabeth, "and then we said okay, it's got to be longer than that!"

On the wedding day, Elizabeth and two seamstresses dressed the bride and admired her composure. "But when she saw herself in the mirror," said one seamstress, "she cried." Everyone panicked when it seemed the massive gown would barely fit into the wedding coach. The twenty five foot train was badly crushed *en route* to the cathedral but quickly straightened under its own weight once the bride alighted.

Lining the procession route was one of the largest crowds London had ever seen. In the glass coach, father and daughter kidded each other.

"More people here," said the Earl, "than at Wembley stadium."

"Oh daddy, when were you ever at Wembley Stadium ?" said Diana.

" Hmmm . . . actually, never."

As always, Diana had to please both her divorced parents. She wore the Spencer family tiara and the Fermoy family's diamond cluster earrings. Kneeling, whispering with Charles at the altar, she forgot any qualms and found herself falling in love again. "I remember being so in love with my husband that I couldn't take my eyes off him . . . I was the luckiest girl in the world," she told Andrew Morton. "I had tremendous hopes in my heart." Crowds outside cheered the couple's amplified vows. Few can have realised though, to what extent the Princess had already fulfilled the promises contained in the hymn she chose for that day. The lyrics were still more poignant sixteen years later at her funeral:

I vow to thee my country - all earthly things above -
entire and whole and perfect, the service of my love,
the love that asks no questions; the love that stands the test,
That lays upon the altar, the dearest and the best:
The love that never falters, the love that pays the price,
The love that makes undaunted the final sacrifice.
Cecil Spring Rice

Thirty percent fantastic . . . and seventy percent sheer slog

Diana in 1982, describing her new life

arl Spencer lamented: "I'm afraid I'll never see my daughter again, you know. They fix his (Charles') schedule two years in advance." After the honeymoon on the Royal Yacht *Britannia*, the newlyweds disappeared into the Balmoral heather. The Spencers would not see Diana for months. After a short stay at Broadlands, the country seat of Earl Mountbatten, Charles and Diana had flown to board *Britannia* at Gibraltar. *En route*, the groom had piloted the aircraft, while neat-as-a-pin Diana found a hoover and vacuumed the passenger cabin. Sailing from Gibraltar, they were alone at last – with about 270 crew, bandsmen and personal staff – for two weeks. The Mediterranean lapped away their pre-nuptial stress as they snorkeled, wind-surfed and lazed. While Charles napped, Diana explored the ship in her bikini. Thus attired, she arrived on the bridge and the crew were barely able to concentrate. She wandered into the shower room and an officer blushed "I'm afraid you should not be here,

ma'am." "Oh, I'm a married woman now," she blushed back.

    The Mediterranean voyage was Diana's first taste of a sybaritic lifestyle she adored almost every summer from then on. In the last two months of her life, she enjoyed no less than four luxury cruises. By comparison, Balmoral is not everybody's idea of heaven. But hidden in Queen Victoria's huge Scottish estate, the royals truly feel untouchable for over two months every year. As summer waned, Diana learned the rudiments of being royal. She and Charles penned 1,250 thank-you letters for Duchy of Cornwall tenants who had subscribed to their wedding present.

    Now the third-ranking royal lady and the most prominent woman on earth, Diana must have found it a jolt to be lowest on the family totem at Balmoral. She had professed the Highlands "magical" a year before, but Balmoral's rustic ways now seemed a stultifying life sentence. Her honeymoon tan faded in the Highland haze. While the Windsors adore fending for themselves at family barbecues, Diana wanted to stay indoors with a dish of mashed potatoes. She needed frank advice about her job but courtiers treated her with isolating deference. "They hung on my every word," Diana told a friend. "Only, I had none . . ." The informal Diana was now " Your Highness." Staff bowed and curtsied. Photographers who had jostled at Coleherne Court, kept a respectful distance during the newlyweds' Highland photocall. Even friends adopted chilling formality. "Don't call me ma'am, call me Duch," she entreated them. Her bulimia continued in full force. Still at Balmoral, she was treated for

The couple spent their wedding night at Broadlands, the Hampshire home of the Mountbatten family and then flew to Gibraltar to join the royal yacht *Britannia* (facing page and above) for a Mediterranean cruise. The next morning the yacht was sailing south of the Balearic Islands – the honeymoon had begun in earnest. The couple lazed on the decks or spent time looking for strange and exotic beaches. The coast of Sardinia came and went, soon they were sailing among the islands of the Aegean Sea. The Royal honeymooners wanted privacy and they found beaches that could only be reached by boat. From Rhodes, the Royal yacht reached the entrance of the Suez Canal, and Egypt. When President Sadat of Egypt and his English-born wife, Juhan, were invited on board for dinner they invited the couple to come back another time to see the wonders of Egypt. The yacht brought the Royal couple to the Red Sea before they were flown, from an Egyptian military airfield, to Balmoral. The official honeymoon was over. (Previous page) London, March 1982. A stunning and pregnant Princess of Wales at the Barbican.

The bedroom given to the Royal couple during the first few days of the honeymoon at Broadlands, Hampshire, (above) the home of Earl Mountbatten, Prince Philip's uncle. Prince Charles considered the Earl a surrogate grandfather and a great friend and had been distraught when he was killed by an IRA bomb in his boat off the Irish coast in 1979. (Facing page) August 19, 1981. The famous hand kissing. To reward the press, knowing that they had had no chance to catch up with the couple during their cruise, the Prince agreed to a photo-call on the banks of the River Dee near Balmoral Castle where they were spending the second part of the honeymoon. Diana looked radiant and happy and when one of the reporters gave her a bunch of flowers she showed her cheeky sense of humour saying "I guess these came out of your expenses".

depression. The Wales' London home was Kensington Palace. Here Diana started working life in the "Family Firm" and acquired ladies-in-waiting and courtiers. She learned that, from now on, every event in her life would be scheduled six months ahead. She claimed that even Prince William's birth was induced to comply with polo schedules! A casual shopping trip became a strategic operation. Shoemaker Manolo Blahnik compared her first and subsequent visits to his shop: "The first time, she came on a bicycle . . . after the wedding, she came by car, with her driver, and we would empty the shop and close up while she was with us."

Dinners were not the pot-luck events of her flat-sharing days. When she longed for baked beans on toast, she suffered in formal dress at some endless banquet. ("Too many long dinners — yuck!" she told a girlfriend.) The girl who refused parts in her school plays learned she must make speeches. Rising to the occasion for the first time during her first Wales trip with Charles, she delivered a maiden address in a rapid schoolgirl gabble. Thunderous applause. Barely 20 years old, she learned to wear hats as religiously as Windsor dowagers. Her first millinery mentor was John Boyd, who saw the Princess as "a poor wee lassie, dressing up in her mother's clothes." Boyd told me that Diana once tried on the Prime Minister's *chapeaux* and did an hilarious Margaret Thatcher impersonation. "We let her play with the hats," he said. "I thought, enjoy yourself while you can."

On early engagements, she made her share of gaffes. Giggling during the national anthem at the Braemar Games earned a scolding. Wanting to match the formal coiffure worn for State Openings of Parliament, she

(Facing page) May 1982. A heavily pregnant Diana at the Guards Polo Club at Windsor. (Right) At the same event with her mother-in-law. Diana always had great respect and affection for the Queen. Perhaps the only time she felt let down was when, during her marital difficulties, the Queen took Charles' side assuming that all the couple problems were due to Diana's bulimia illness.
(Below) Christmas 1981. Outside St George's Chapel at Windsor. Diana, pregnant with William, chatting to her seventeen year-old brother-in-law Edward at one of the few occasions in the year when the Royals, young and old, are together.

Diana, in a pink maternity dress, chatting with her husband at polo. Diana was determined not let let Charles feel let down and tried to be with him in spite of suffering from morning sickness.
(Facing page) June 21, 1982. A Royal birth. Diana and Charles on the steps of Paddington St Mary's with their new baby, William. Diana had a hard time during the delivery and at one point the consultant, Mr Pinker, considered an emergency caesarean — but finally she was able to give birth by her own efforts. By 9.03 pm, she was a happy mother. Again at polo (below) with Sarah Ferguson, her future sister-in-law. Diana wore the same maternity outfit when she left St Mary's after the birth of William.

Diana **92** *an English rose*

November 1984. Remembrance Sunday: Diana and Princess Anne on the balcony in Whitehall. Two months after the birth of her second son, Diana was very thin.

(Below) A sunny day in 1984, at Sandrigham with Charles and the Royal Family for the annual Christmas Day service in happier days. Diana, always fashion conscious, did not just wear warm clothes and here wears a red military coat with black buttons by Piero de Monzi. After the separation from Charles, in 1992, Diana attended the Sandrigham church service only once for the sake of her children. Finding the occasion too painful and uncomfortable she chose to spend a lonely Christmas at Kensington Palace.

(Facing page) September 1982. Princess Grace of Monaco had died in a car accident and Diana went straight to the Queen and gained her approval to attend the Princess's funeral — after a "No" from the Queen's private secretary. This first solo trip abroad gained her praise for her dignified manner.

Bulimia attacks were very frequent in the period between Diana's two pregnancies. Rumours in the press mistook her illness for anorexia. Throughout, Diana forced herself to show a happy face in public. She was tormented with the thought of her husband having a liaison with Camilla and the birth of William was followed by post-natal depression. She saw several doctors and psychologists, but she lacked the will to help herself. (Right) November 1982. Diana with Charles and Princess Margaret welcoming Queen Beatrix of Holland, in London for her state visit. Diana was terribly fond of "auntie" Margaret. (Above) At a gala dinner at Guildhall, London in 1982. Looking gaunt and staring at an empty plate, this is a very unhappy Diana. (Facing page) A stunning, but thin, Princess of Wales during the Royal couple's Australian tour in 1983.

commissioned an upswept hair style. When newspaper editors gave the new hairdo more news coverage than her mother-in-law's speech, Diana was seen as an upstaging prima donna. At the time, she described her job as "thirty per cent fantastic and seventy per cent sheer slog."

Years later, she would tell Andrew Morton of rampant bulimia, fights with Charles about Camilla Parker-Bowles and cry-for-help suicide attempts. She was skin and bone. John Boyd scolded Diana for her thinness. "It's called slim, Mr Boyd," she replied. "My husband prefers me this way." Indeed, their London staff called Kensington Palace "Biafra" because both Charles and Diana were skeletal.

Stress came from all quarters. The Queen had reassured Diana that public hunger for her would soon wane. But something in her freshness had induced an addiction in the masses. They wanted more. Thin and sick, she was exhausted by the constant clamour. In Wales, she sobbed in the car, unable to face the crowds who cried "Diana, Diana!" Yet, while in their frenzied midst, she was a model of smiling composure. Years earlier, the Queen Mother had summed up the phenomenon the new girl was experiencing: "I must admit that sometimes (in a crowd) I feel something flow out of me," the Queen Mother said. " It makes me feel very tired for a moment. Then I seem to get something back . . . and I feel strength again. In fact, recharged."

(Facing page) The Prince and Princess of Wales during their visit to Barmouth in Wales in November, 1982. Diana, at such an early stage in her married life, was an instant success. She made contact with people, rarely wore gloves and showed her tender touch with children. The Welsh people immediately took this young girl to their heart.
(Above) A cheeky banner from schoolchildren who waited to catch a glimpse of the Princess.

Diana claimed that smiling through anguish was an inherited skill. As a child, she had seen her mother feign serenity after violent rows. "However bloody you are feeling," the Princess told Andrew Morton, "you can put on the most amazing show of happiness." Bulimia experts cite this type of facade as a textbook symptom of the eating disorder. By the end of 1982, she really did have a reason to smile. Diana was pregnant and in the words of the Pop Princess, " absolutely over the moon."

Stepping from the 'plane at Alice Springs, in 1983, Diana stood brushing flies from her face. I thought how thin and awkward she looked: shoulders drooping, eyes blinking in the harsh sunlight. Then her nanny handed 21-year-old Diana the infant William. What an instant change! She was now straight-backed and confident, as if nothing in the gruelling weeks that lay ahead could daunt her. The baby gave her strength and purpose. And William and Harry adored their mother. Among all the sights at Diana's funeral, none was more touching than her sons' final letter, propped on the coffin. No title bestowed by the masses better suited Diana than the single word on the envelope holding their last message, "Mummy."

Diana questioned her achievements as a Princess but she knew she did not fail her sons. Neither could the sternest Palace critics fault her there. In a live speech before Diana's funeral, the Queen said she admired and respected

Kensington Palace May 1983: Delightful pictures of a playful Prince William with his doting parents. Curiosity got the better of the toddler when he started to inspect one of the TV crews' video cameras.
(Facing page) 1982. At six months, a wonderful portrait of mother and baby.

the Princess, "especially for her devotion to her two boys". If Diana's own childhood often lacked a mother' arms, she became a living proponent for her own "children-need-hugs" mantra. Her close friend Rosa Monckton wrote: "I remember Prince Harry coming through the door of her study . . . launching himself like a projectile into her arms." Lana Marks, a Palm Beach fashion designer, remembers: "Diana would drop everything whenever her boys came home from school. It didn't matter which head of state she had to see or what gala she had to attend. Those were secondary."

As a new bride of the Eighties, the desire to instantly provide heirs put Diana at odds with her generation. But it much recommended the 19 year-old to the Windsors when she claimed: "I want lots and lots of children . . . I want to rival Queen Victoria!" She revised that view after her difficult first pregnancy and delivery. At Tetbury a man asked if she was again expecting. "You must be joking, " she shot back. "I'm not on a production line!" All the same, through her chequered royal career, Diana saw motherhood as her first duty.

During a 1984 blizzard, she refused to cancel a visit to cot-death parents in Cambridge. "I'm a mother," she explained. "So I had to come." She championed her children's right to as normal an upbringing as possible. Diana not only breast-fed both boys, she raised society eyebrows by speaking out for the practice. If William cried during the night, Diana usually beat the nanny to his bedside. On walkabout, I heard her tell an Australian mum: "I'm having trouble sleeping because of (William's) teething – I do get tired." She said she would gladly change places with another Aussie mum to be able to stay home with her baby. ("She must be mad," the woman said later.) Floella Benjamin, a TV presenter, was herself a new parent in 1982 when Diana raved about William's baby skin and admitted "ooh, I want to bite his botty!"

The royal mother broke precedents at every turn. She said she frequently slept with her sons. Before Christmas, she took the boys to department stores and made them line up to see Santa. Diana insisted on every stage of their education being outside Palace walls. But it was her hand they clutched on their first trip to the classroom and it was mummy who often drove them to school. Diana usually arrived for sports days and parents' teas. When William was accidentally bashed in the skull at school with a golf club, Diana stayed at his hospital bed overnight – Charles went to the opera. Aware of her eldest son's sensitive nature, she was hell-bent that he should not follow his father and Prince Phillip to Gordonstoun in Scotland. (Charles, who hated the school, did not argue.) In 1995, William donned the Victorian tail coat uniform of Charles Spencer's *alma mater*, Eton. Three years later, brother Harry would also enter its hallowed portals.

Although Diana was once seen to slap William's bottom at a school sports day, she was not overly strict. Young William was famously fond of flushing his papa's handmade shoes down the loo. Peter Settelen, Diana's speech coach, told me he tried to video her interview technique when the boys were home from school in 1993. "They were irritated that mummy was working so they kept finding reasons to interrupt us." Settelen questioned Diana as the camera rolled and the little princes imitated her replies in silly voices. "The session ended," laughs Settelen, "when Prince William broke wind loudly next to her. She was, after all, a mother first and a princess second."

Fearing they would later endure enough discipline, she could seldom bring herself to scold her sons. But Diana made sure they did not use their position to walk over ordinary folk. On a visit to a theatre, Harry asked a worker for regular water and complained when he was given the fizzy stuff. "That's the sort of behaviour that gives the Royal Family a bad name," Diana berated the 12 year-old. Her friend Lord Archer, author and politician, said the Princess didn't want her sons "to go through life thinking, 'you're a member of the Royal Family and that's how you live all the time'." But she was particularly aware that William had this role to play, that she was the mother of the future king.

She was not without humour on the subject, though. Singer Sir Cliff Richard commented on William's height and predicted the boy would have a super tennis serve. Diana, a great mimic, pronounced in Victorian tones: "There is more to being a monarch, Sir Cliff, than having a great serve." A great handshake is preferable. Diana started William off on a lifetime of flesh-pressing before he was six. In red silk shorts, he stood beside his mother and offered his palm to 180 delegates at a fashion writers' convention. "It's good practice for him," said his mother, "though he did get a little fed up towards the end." Later, Diana encouraged both sons to make little speeches at Palace staff parties and to look squarely into strangers' eyes on

1984. Polo at Windsor, and Diana is pregnant with Harry. (Facing page) The pregnant Princess in pale blue trousers and pink sweater. She confided later to Andrew Morton that during her pregnancy with Harry, her relationship with her husband had never been better – and that she found this quite ironic, as she suspected that once again Charles was seeing Camilla.

walkabouts with their mother. She could hardly have known she was preparing them for their first and hardest walkabouts without her. All too soon, at 15 and 13 years old, William and Harry were obliged to walk among strangers and accept condolences on their mother's death.

Experience would somewhat inure them to press attention, yet Diana was known to fight like a tiger for her son's privacy. When *paparazzi* outside Kensington Palace tried to snap William as she drove him to school, Diana rolled down her window and screamed: "Leave him alone! Alone, do you hear! How would you like your children to be treated like that?" Even within the cloisters of Eton, William had to be somewhat shielded from his parents' escapades. Rumours and admissions of infidelities were rife when, on a 1996 prize day, a series of speeches on the deadly sins had "lust" edited out. School officials thought references to adultery might be uncomfortable for William's parents. In 1997, William asked mummy and papa to stay home from the event.

Diana's friend Liz Tilberis says: "When William went to Eton, she was terribly worried about him being hounded by the press. She was trying so hard

to teach her sons how to cope with media attention. William saw how the press treated her. He understood her fury with them and he also understood that she courted them . . . he was very close to his mother and was full of sympathy for her." The boys suffered for both parents during the downward spiral towards divorce. Pathetically, they even tried to make things better. Harry insisted mummy and daddy should hold hands while the family was together. When Diana sobbed in her bathroom, William pushed tissues under the door.

Beyond her own miseries, Diana wanted both sons to share her compassion for the down-trodden. When she felt they were ready, she took them to homeless shelters and AIDS hospices. "Through learning what I do and what his father does, (William) has got an insight into what is coming his way," said Diana. "He's not hidden upstairs with the governess." Just as Diana had done in her teens, the elder Prince helped entertain mentally handicapped children who visited his prep school. Diana was "thrilled and proud." "A lot of adults couldn't handle that," she said. "Britain will be lucky to get William.

September 15, 1984. Prince Harry was born on a Saturday at 4.20 pm at Paddington St Mary's Hospital, as was big brother William. A scan had shown that she was expecting a boy and, knowing how desperate her husband was for a girl, Diana kept this news a secret. When Charles saw the baby, Diana thought he looked disappointed and made a remark about his Spencer red hair. Then he left to go and play polo. "Something inside me died," she was said to have told a friend.

(Top) 1985. The Queen's official birthday and the Royal family gather on the Palace balcony after Trooping The Colour. (Above and left) 1986. Derby day. The Princess of Wales in a smart outfit with Charles and her father-in-law Prince Philip. (Facing page) 1985. In a chic, black-and-white silk dress which she enjoyed wearing at official engagements or at the Guards Polo Club. Diana was adept at wearing the same outfit on more than one occasion — to refresh the look she would change hair styles and wear different jewellery.

(Facing page) January 1987. First day at Wetherby School for young William. Diana was a caring mother and whenever her commitments allowed her she took her children to school.

(Left)1991. Both children were reunited with their parents during the Wales' State Visit to Canada. The tensions in the relationship were beginning to show, but Diana was delighted to be with William and Harry again.

He's all right." In the 1995 BBC interview, she told Martin Bashir: "I want them to have an understanding of people's emotions, people's insecurities, people's distress and people's hopes and dreams."

Though the mother taught her sons to show affection for each other, boys would be boys. At Kensington Palace, Harry asked a visiting brother and sister if they ever fought. "Of course," they replied. Harry looked greatly relieved and said "Good, because my brother and I fight all the time." Once witnessing the absurd comedy of Charles ordering masses of refreshments at a polo match and offering a single pound note as payment, Diana put the boys on a weekly allowance so they might early learn the value of money. There were other economies. As he sprouted to over six feet by the age of 16, William's trouser legs showed evidence of multiple letdowns. Harry got his cast-offs. The same pastel blue coat that William wore one Easter was trotted out by Harry two Easters later.

Diana had no ordinary life after leaving Coleherne Court, but she had

Diana's greatest joy was to take her boys out to have fun and (facing page) in April, 1992 she enjoyed a splashing time with Harry at Thorpe Park. (Above) March 9, 1997. The official portrait of the Royal Family on the day of Prince William's confirmation at Windsor Castle, taken in the White Drawing Room. (Front row) Prince Harry, Prince William, with Charles, Diana and the Queen. Behind, from left to right, King Constantine of Greece, Lady Susan Hussey, Princess Alexandra, the Duchess of Westminster and Lord Romsey. A relaxed and smiling Diana showed that by then she was more at peace with Charles, enjoying her independence and fulfillment in her new life as an unofficial ambassador for Britain.

not forgotten its joys. Incognito with his mother and brother, William became the first King-in-waiting to patronise fast food franchises. The Princes wore sweat shirts and baseball caps to pop concerts and visited theme parks, where a screaming Diana clung to them on the water rides. She took them go-karting. She told her friend Mary Robertson of her wish to give the boys a "normal" life. "My husband thinks I'm over-doing it," she added. But a rainy-day trip to the cinema could become a political nightmare. Thinking she was simply taking the boys to a Brad Pitt movie in 1997, Diana found herself rebuked in the press when the film turned out to sympathise with the IRA. She issued a fast apology. But the positive aspect was that thanks to Diana, William and Harry did experience public cinemas; that they did rub shoulders with others waiting for rides at Disney World. One wonders if they ever will again.

At her funeral, her brother Charles promised Diana that "your blood family will do all we can to continue the imaginative way in which you were steering these two exceptional young men so that their souls are not simply immersed by duty and tradition but can sing openly as you planned . . . we, like you, recognise the need for them to experience as many aspects of life as possible to arm them . . . for the years ahead." Spencer was hinting at Diana's last will and testament, which would be published months later. Written in 1993, the document showed she disapproved of Windsor child-raising. She not only wanted her mother and brother to be guardians, Diana left specific instructions that her mother should participate in her sons' upbringing. Diana's will also showed a mother's concern for the Princes' material welfare. The bulk of her £35.6 million estate – £21.3 million after taxes – was left to William and Harry.

As a very young man, William professed the ambition "to be a policeman, so that I can look after you, mummy." Probably not as a policeman, William will nevertheless get his chance. In as much as people loved Diana, they will see the actions of her sons as her most personal legacy. And in becoming compassionate individuals who "sing openly" as Diana planned, they will be able to protect the legacy of "mummy" as long as they live.

Diana is so bonnie
she would look lovely
in a dish rag.

John Boyd, milliner

It was not an auspicious start. Diana wondered if she would go down in history as "the girl who forgot her petticoat." For her first photo-call, she wore a voile skirt and stood with the sun behind her. On ensuing front pages, all Britain marvelled at her legs. Charles conceded "I knew your legs were good . . . I didn't realise they were that spectacular." Fifteen years and a million photographs later, fashion designers would agree. "Even among models," said Karl Lagerfeld, "there are no legs like this."

At 19, Diana owned skirts, jeans and sweaters. But before she was even a fiancée, commentary on Diana's wardrobe had begun. Nor would it stop after she died, buried in a black Catherine Walker coat dress she had chosen from the '97 collection but had not had a chance to wear. Her grief-stricken butler took it to Paris and dressed his boss for her journey home.

Two months later, in the wild west of America, I found icons in the form

(Right and above) 1985. A beautiful dark blue velvet dress with a deep cut-out in the bodice, front and back, filled with lace panels, designed by Catherine Walker. To complement the dress, a diamond and sapphire choker over a velvet ribbon. (Facing page) Another Catherine Walker creation, blue silk chiffon draped around the waist to form a crossover yoke. With matching chiffon stole, Diana wore this dress at the Cannes Film Festival in 1987. Sold at Christie's auction in 1997. (Previous page) A pale blue chiffon evening dress, by Catherine Walker.

(Left) June 1997. Diana visited the Shri Swaminarayan Mandir Hindu Temple, in Neasden, London and wore a Catherine Walker cream double-breasted dress.

(Below left) Auckland, New Zealand 1983. Gina Fratini dressed Diana in a creamy organza and satin gown. Very delicate lacework at the front of the bodice and large puffed transparent sleeves.

(Below right) 1995. VE day celebrations. A charming straw hat to keep cool complemented by a beautiful pastel coloured suit.

Facing page: (Top left) The Peak District 1987. The Princess of Wales at the First Festival of National Parks held at Chatsworth Park — delicate lace collar and cuffs for this tartan wool dress by Bellville Sassoon.

(Bottom left) By Jacques Azagury. 1920s-style chiffon gown with velvet effect top, embroidered with stars.

(Right) London,1993.In striking purple and a patterned silk blouse, on a visit to the London Arts Council.

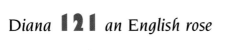

Diana **121** *an English rose*

Indonesia, 1989. The year ended with the Prince and Princess visiting Indonesia and Hong Kong. Diana had a chance to show her compassion when she visited the Sitanala Leprosy Hospital on the outskirts of Jakarta. No gloves, she shook hands with and touched many of the leprosy victims. At a reception (right) she wore this wonderful silk blue dress — two decorative buttons its only accessory. Diana by then had become less fussy, avoiding too many frills. (Facing page) May 1995. Visiting the 2nd battalion of the Queen's and Royal Hampshire regiment, Diana wore Gianni Versace's "Jackie Kennedy" suit, combining glamour and formality. Diana's solo trip to the Argentine in the same year saw Versace's pastiche re-used.

of Diana's gowns. At a shopping mall – where young girls outfit themselves for under $30 – stood a Victor Edelstein *circa* 1988 evening gown I had once seen on Diana. Lunch hour crowds gathered around the ghostly form, marvelling at Diana's height and svelteness. As if the gown were a holy relic, some Dianaphiles left flowers at its hem.

At the Christie's auction five months before, the Romance Classics Television Network had bid £55,000 (a sum close to what Diana paid for it) to own this exquisite souvenir of the world's best-dressed woman. Richly encrusted with gems in Empire design, the gown was made to grace the salons of the Elysée Palace for President Mitterand's banquet. As if to prove it had been worn by a real person, a few rhinestones were missing from the bolero's back. I could almost smell her perfume. I realised we would never see style like Diana's again . . . and I felt like crying.

In sixteen years, we saw her in so many beautiful clothes that it was hard to imagine her without a single long gown when she courted Charles. Just before her betrothal, she and her mother had pondered the suit section at Harrods. They chose a blue suit for her official photo debut. The idea was to complement her sapphire ring. But the ensemble was not made for a teenager; it would have better suited Mrs Shand Kydd . . . or Margaret Thatcher.

Her first designer gown, bought for Diana's first engagement with Charles, fared poorly with critics. "It was a horrendous occasion," she confided. Charles did not approve the décolletage of the Emanuel crinoline, or the colour black (his clan wore it only for funerals). "Black to me was the smartest colour you could possibly have at the age of 19," Diana explained. But the real problem was the off-the-rack bodice. It kept slipping down, much to the delight of the press. "I was quite big-chested then," said Diana. "They all got frightfully excited."

Newspapers again showed more of Diana than she planned. Like many of her early purchases, that dress was never worn again. She had height, a great shape, but with clothes, she needed advice. Anna Harvey at *Vogue* magazine filled an office with super clothes and invited Diana over. "Her eyes lit up when she saw all the racks – I don't think she had any idea how many lovely things there were out there," says Ms Harvey.

Argentinian Roberto Devoirik, who handles Lacroix in London, was called to help. In the *Vogue* editor's office, he saw "this schoolgirl called Diana Spencer. I was told she was going to get married to the Prince of Wales . . . the poor girl was thrown into a pond of silks and cashmeres. The people at *Vogue* would tell her to wear this and that." But mistakes were frequent. For Diana's first ever Royal Ascot, Benny Ong created a delicious peach-sundae suit and flounced blouse. Some time later, Jasper Conran no doubt

Australia, Melbourne, 1985. At the Botanical Garden Diana wore a red coat by Jan Vanvelden, over a polka dot dress.

(Facing page) Paris, 1988. Diana at Orly airport on arrival for the Wales's five-day visit to France. Dressed by Chanel, Karl Lagerfeld designed this red coat, worn over a white silk blouse and black skirt. Also by Chanel, the small hat with feather at the side — her way of paying tribute to their hosts, she looked terribly French.

winced to see the same blouse cluttering his white gabardine ensemble. Bruce Oldfield's salon was a mecca for Diana. He recalled of the early Eighties: "She was buying from too many designers and mixing indiscriminately. She went off on the fashion world like a loose cannon – a kid in a candy shop. One day a big gown, the next a horrible, fussy hat." Fortunately, as milliner John Boyd told me, "Diana is so bonnie she would look lovely in a dish rag."

Inspired by fashion's "Neo Romantic" period, Diana – star of the romance of the century – naturally became patron saint for the masses. She was copied slavishly as the "Lady Di look" encircled the globe. Wearing low heels so as not to dwarf her Prince, she made "flatties" a worldwide rage. But she wallowed in the design deep-end, sporting too many flounces. Too many fancy necklines. Too many polka dots. Rows of pearls above too fussy collars. Bows were her worst excess. They cluttered her hats, shoulders, waist and *derrière*. They clung to her wrists, hosiery, shoes and most famously at the breast of the bouffant Emanuel wedding gown.

New York, 1996. A new hairstyle for a new dress, blue silk crepe with built-in-corset. This hairstyle was another "miss" for her critics. Diana did not use it again. (Facing page) In New York, at the Metropolitan Museum in 1996, Diana wore Dior for the first time. The dress was designed by John Galliano. The beautiful navy blue slip dress also was not acclaimed by the media.

By the Nineties she hated pictures of her Eighties wardrobe. Roberto Devoirik asked: "What happened to the wedding dress?" She said: "I hope the moths eat it a bit and reduce the volume." Less picky, guests at Althorp's museum in 1998 gasped at the historic silken meringue. "Much lovelier than I remembered," said a woman who had travelled from California for the close encounter. "But the colour seemed duller after 17 years."

Assembling a trousseau was a huge project for the bride and her mother. Diana recalled: "We had to go out and buy six of everything and we still didn't have enough . . . you have to change four times a day and suddenly your wardrobe expands to something unbelievable. Hence, probably, the criticism when I first arrived on the scene of having new clothes all the time."

For a good part of her first royal years, she filled out prettily in maternity dresses. But the first pregnancy caught the young bride unprepared. Dressing to turn on the Regent Street Christmas lights, she could not close the zip on her velvet culottes. She somehow survived the event with hands clamped to her waistband, stopping the pants from descending!

After the babies, it was back to fussy ensembles for tours. Only years later did she and Catherine Walker discover the understated magnificence of a column dress on a supermodel figure. As she overcame bulimia and built a more solid shape, concealing ensembles were ditched for the short, power suits that became a latter-day trademark. Still later, retreating from public duties, Diana gleefully adopted the pared-down sexiness of Versace, Armani and Lacroix. By then, she could use foreign labels. As Princess of Wales on parade, she had to buy the very best of British. But she made an exception for her first visit to France. Embarrassed by her schoolgirlish French,

(Below) A John Galliano trouser suit. This jacket was also worn with a matching skirt. It is now, with other Diana garments, on show at Althorp.
(Right) London, 1981 a "James Bond" film premiere. Young, in love and full of dreams, Diana chose this dress, in gold silk chiffon by Bellville Sassoon.
(Facing page) London 1992. Diana took her boys, in this off-the-shoulder fuschia dress to a Christmas carol concert.

Diana **129** *an English rose*

(Left and above) April, 1985.
A glamourous evening gown in gold lamé, at a dinner given by her dress designer, Bruce Oldfield, in aid of Dr. Barnardo's.
Facing page: (Main picture)
A stunning evening gown worn in 1986 in Muscat, Oman – ivory satin with a lace bodice, designed by the Emanuels.
(Top) The Emanuels' black and white duchess satin gown worn during the Middle East tour in 1985.
(Below) Lilac silk taffeta evening gown, worn by a young Princess of Wales in New Zealand in 1983, designed by Donald Campbell.

(Right) Arlington National Cemetery in Washington, DC in 1985. Slick and smart, this dress by Bruce Oldfield has a very high waist band and could not have been worn by anybody but the Princess, the perfect model. (Inset) Australia, 1985. Jan Vanvelden dressed Diana in this lovely lilac woollen dress. The dropped waistline with white collar was worn with a small hat by John Boyd. (Facing page) 1987. A gesture of gallantry during the royal couple's visit to Spain. On her arrival at Salamanca, students threw their cloaks on the ground for the Princess to walk on. Diana sports a red and white suite with matching two-tone shoes.

she hit Paris dressed head to toe – and even perfumed – by Chanel. She was speaking French . . . her way.

The fashion ambassadress prepared anxiously for tours. Her mentors haunted Kensington Palace with couturier samples. "We'd sit on the floor of her drawing room, looking at sketches and fabrics, while the butler brought in endless coffee," recalls Anna Harvey. "Once she called her husband into the drawing room to ask what he thought of a black Murray Arbeid dress; he just stared at her in it and said 'you look absolutely wonderful'." Fully aware of of her legend, Diana never fretted about being upstaged, even in the most glitzy crowd. No star

outshone Diana in the gown she carefully chose for the 1985 White House banquet. Anna Harvey was in on the selection: "She knew that the midnight blue dress by Victor Edelstein, which she wore when she danced with John Travolta . . . was one heck of a number and it thrilled her."

She developed an instinct for daring but untrashy gowns. In those signature one-shouldered gowns, she could be sexy while baring nothing more than a tanned arm. She wore her first – a Hachi creation in white – for six years, at last selling it at the Christie's auction. Diana continued the same asymmetric gimmick in gowns by other designers. The last was a white Versace, never publicly worn, which was displayed at Althorp.

Often witty in her

selections, she chose a bare-backed velvet gown for the *Back to the Future* premiere and swung a rope of knotted pearls down her spine. For another formal gig, she and Charles both arrived in tuxedos. An amusing idea in accessorising was to team a red and black gown with one red and one black glove. When Richard Branson of Virgin Airlines invited her to christen his new airliner "Lady in Red", she mischievously showed up in . . . well, green.

Diana's greatest clothing genius was in suiting her look to compliment her situation. For a "Swan Lake" performance, she found a fairy-like Elizabeth Emanuel ballerina dress. At the Cannes film festival, she wore an ice-blue chiffon which became known as the "Grace Kelly". The royal visitor applauded Thailand

1987. Welcoming King Fahd of Saudi Arabia, at Gatwick airport, in a Royal Hussar-style suit by Catherine Walker. Hat by Graham Smith at Kangol. (Facing page) Australia, Perth 1983. At a garden party at Government House Diana wore this icy-blue suit, looking like a little sailor, by Catherine Walker.

(Left) Casually dressed in a smart striped dress at a polo match. Charles' enthusiasm for polo ensured that, in the early years of their marriage, Diana found herself spending a lot of time as a spectator at the polo field.

(Inset) Australia 1985. Flowers for a Princess. Deep plum dress, wide belt and a white collar with a large hat to match, by Catherine Walker and Frederick Fox.

(Facing page) Madrid, 1987. An emerald green dress with white trimmings by Catherine Walker with a stunning hat with a large brim by Peter Somerville.

(Inset) By the same designer, a black lace dress with a lace veil in the same fabric for a special meeting with His Holiness, Pope John Paul, at the Vatican during their Italian visit.

with Catherine Walker's sarong-style gown. She reigned in Spain with Murray Arbeid's fabulous flamenco number. She was wonderful in tartan at the Braemar Games. She wore trade-mark sailor hats to anything vaguely nautical. The feminine lines of Pakistan's *Shalwar Kameez* so flattered the Princess that she took the style back to London, where it instantly became high fashion. When she gelled and slicked back her hair for a fashion award gala in New York, British papers ran stories on how to achieve "Diana's wet look." Though royal visitors must avoid politics, she could wordlessly salute a host nation by wearing its flag. So successful was her red and green "Welsh flag" outfit on her honeymoon tour in 1981, that Diana repeated the idea with a red spotted "rising sun" hat and dress in Japan. Her smartest coup was in Edmonton, where the jagged puritan collar of her Vanvelden under-blouse fell like a maple leaf flag across her red suit. Oh, Canada!

Gowns designed for grand occasions, like Catherine Walker's "Elvis" or the white Edelstein I encountered on its tour of Californian shopping malls, were so distinctive that they could not be worn more than a few times. So when Diana cleaned out for charity in 1997, she really needed the closet space. After her first six years as Princess of Wales, Diana owned 144 formal gowns, 80 suits and 50 day outfits! There is a royal technique to recycle often-worn finery. A gown that has had too many British outings makes a comeback in some Commonwealth outpost. The concealing dresses that Catherine Walker designed for Diana's Arab States visits would reappear in London, streamlined to reveal knees, shoulders and bosom.

When Diana became embroiled in serious issues, she resented the clothes-horse image. Pointedly on her Bosnian land mines visit, she did not wash or style her hair and was seldom out of jeans. On tours in the Nineties, she ceased providing press releases about each change of clothes. The emphasis of media attention should be on her work, not her dresses. Still, Diana never quite relinquished her passion for lovely, attention-getting clothes. Without the "Her Royal Highness" title, she snubbed royal convention and revealed her tan in movie-star sheaths. She paraded *femme-fatale* gowns of forbidden black. Backs got lower, which sometimes presented a problem for gentlemen hosts who nudged her politely along from behind. "They never know where to put their hands," Diana giggled. Hemlines inched up. At French designer Roland Klein's salon, she studied her dress and commanded: "Shorter, shorter! Whatever I wear, I'll be criticised, so let's go for it!"

Diana bravely experimented with a lingerie look, slithering into John Galliano's £10,000 navy slip for a New York benefit. Too late, Diana realised it was not best to boogie bra-less and slipped away from the ball without dancing a step. In an azure Jacques Azagury cocktail mini worn to the Royal Albert Hall just before she died, Diana paraded the show-stopping allure of the dress that is at

The bodice of this Empire-style dress, is embroidered to emulate Mughal embroidery. By Catherine Walker. (Facing page) An elegant evening gown, in fuschia pink silk by Victor Edelstein. Both auctioned at Christie's in 1997.

A dazzling gold and red gown by Bruce Oldfield and (below) a night at the theatre in 1986. Over a satin blouse a navy jacket, enriched by sequins, by Jan Vanvelden. Facing page: (Top) Padded shoulders, a pink crushed-velvet dress, by Catherine Walker. Worn in 1985 the gown is rushed up the front. (Bottom) By the same designer, a burgundy velvet gown with plunging back and worn with long strands of knotted pearls — or simply with nothing. However she wore it, Diana always looked a million dollars.

(Right) Washington DC, 1985. Ivory taffeta and lace, this wonderful drop-waisted gown with scalloped neckline was designed by Murray Arbeid. The Queen Mary tiara adds the final touch.

(Above) One-sleeved silk taffeta dress, printed with hazy red roses by Catherine Walker. Worn in Paris in 1988.

Facing page: (Top left) Paris. Haute couture by Victor Edelstein. This evening gown was made for a would-be Queen. The work was so elaborate that the Princess chose to wear simply a pair of earrings, a gift from the Emir of Qatar.

(Top right) Norway, 1984. At the gala of *Carmen* given by the London City Ballet, Diana in a red duchess satin gown, with a separate laced bolero top, Jan Vanvelden. (Bottom) By Catherine Walker — a simple, sleeky, tight fitting dress that is cut to the waist at the back with a lace insert.

once very short, and very scooped in front and back. Azagury softened the racy impact by stitching neat bows to the shoulder straps "There was always a sexy aspect to her dressing," remembers the designer. "I was never scared to say, shorter shirt! Lower neckline!"

Apparently, she drew limits. "I would love to wear a dress that's slashed to the waist, but it isn't for me," she told Bruce Oldfield. But in fitting sessions she abandoned modesty, never asking staff to leave the room while she changed. One male designer headed for the door of her sitting room. "She cried 'Stay!'" He blushed. "So I crossed over to the window and stared out fixedly across the park."

The royal client was passionate for detail. Frogging, seed pearls, exquisite lace, rhinestones, bugle beads and sequins were the lavish trademarks of her 16-year reign over European fashion. Catherine Walker's famous "Elvis" outfit was weighed down by 20,000 *faux* pearls, each stitched on by hand. A cocktail dress had cuffs secured by six diamante and pearl buttons, each worth £150! No vainer than the next woman, so perhaps Diana's fashion compulsion harked back to being a lumpy teenager, over-shadowed by her sisters. The mature Princess may also have wanted to sock it to style critics who sneered at her early blunders. Liz Tilberis, who was fashion editor at British *Vogue* when she met the royal fiancée, says the fashion-plate Princess who slowly evolved was Diana's own invention. "Lots of us would love to take credit for her transformation . . . but the truth is, she worked it all out for herself."

As a divorcée, Diana chose clothes which she thought would make her sons proud, her husband regretful, and his mistress puce. She was quietly thrilled after a 1995 Remembrance ceremony, when the tabloids ran front-page comparisons between Mrs Parker-Bowles' get-up for the event and Diana's divine ensemble. A typical Diana trick was dressing to snatch the limelight, particularly if Charles threatened to garner front pages. On the night Charles' famous "adultery" interview was to be televised, she arrived at the Serpentine Gallery in the ultimate black revenge number by Christina Stambolian. Host Lord Palumbo greeted Diana in wonder. "She bounded out of the car in that wonderfully athletic way she has, wearing what the Americans call the 'I'll show you' dress. I have never seen her in better form," he recalls.

Liverpool, 1981. Diana looks like a school girl in uniform, playing at being grown-up. The twenty-year old Princess looks so vulnerable, belying the courage of a young woman taking on the challenge of being the wife of the heir to the throne. (Facing page) October, 1996. Sydney, Australia. Princess Diana wearing a turquoise silk dress caught on one shoulder. Another of the many stunning Versace creations Diana so enjoyed.

Diana loved the power of being the unchallenged, most glamourous and famous person at any event. But it was not just an ego-trip. She knew glamour remained her biggest tool in fund-raising. Says designer Bruce Oldfield: "She committed herself to looking good because it was a way of doing her job well." To the very end, Diana looked on fashion not just as a pleasure but a responsibility. She hated to think people who supported her charities might feel short-changed.

"They'll be disappointed if they see me looking dowdy," she told her hairdresser. "People are expecting Princess Diana."

(Above)
Paris 1991.
Designed
by Viv Knowlands,
this hat, first worn
in 1986, and
complemented by a veil is
appropriately solemn for the occasion
— Remembrance Day.
(Above left) New Zealand,
Auckland,1983. At Government
House, Diana braves the heavy rain
in a white straw hat with black satin
band and bow.
(Left) A beautiful, off-white hat with
creamy edging at the brim and a
wonderful, very neat, two-tone bow
at the front.
(Facing page) Two creations from
milliner John Boyd. (Bottom left).
Australia, 1985. Visiting Mildura,
Diana chose to wear a dainty little
hat with a net over her eyes.
(Above left) Australia, 1983. At an
official ceremony in Perth. Pink
fuschia gathered at one side with a
lovely big bow. (Right, top and
bottom) A red hat for a very young
and happy Princess, and an older, but
still happy, Diana with a straw black
hat with satin band around the large
brim — Diana also wore this to her
father's funeral.

Diana **147** an English rose

India, 1992. A wide brimmed blue and white hat to keep the sun off. Facing page: (Top right). Caen, France 1987. A red woollen suit by Rifat Ozbek accessorised with a large hat by Philip Somerville.

(Top left) John Boyd's hats were a regular accessory for Diana. 1985, with band, turned-up brim and feather trim and (bottom left) Australia, April 1993, a white and red straw hat was combined with a red silk suit by Jan Vanvelden.

(Bottom right) Tasmania, 1983. Again by John Boyd, this time combined with a two piece-suit by Jasper Conran.

Why don't you ask me about the Princess's beautiful blue eyes?

Canadian Prime Minister Pierre Trudeau, 1983

THE Royal Family has a handshake more exclusive than the Freemasons – a secret way to clasp a proffered hand so one's fingers cannot be scrunched. It doesn't always work. After long days of hand-squashing on royal tours, Diana and Charles had to soak their mitts in iced water. No Princess of Wales travelled as much as Diana. By the end of her life, she had seen the pyramids, the Taj Mahal, the White House, the Colosseum and most of the wonders of the ancient and modern world. She had danced with movie stars, sat cross-legged with Emirs, held hands with lepers. She had worn kimonos in Japan, garlands in Nepal and veils in the Vatican.

And no Princess of Wales was ever so adored wherever she went. In the Far East, folk who could not speak English screamed her name like a mantra. In the Middle East, potentates heaped diamonds her way. Countries where royalty was anathema fell at her feet. The finicky French applauded her English clothes. Worldly American celebrities gushed like children. In 1983, Canadian host Prime Minister Pierre Trudeau scolded a reporter for asking him trivial questions. "Why don't you ask me about the Princess's beautiful blue eyes?" he sighed. Portuguese president Mario Soares was reduced to a blushing mess when, in full view of Lisbon's luminaries, Diana twanged his trouser braces. Light as a feather, Diana stepped effortlessly through protocol – even if she was sometimes required to be

Australia, New Zealand March/April 1983. Diana at Alice Springs shows off William (right). (Above and facing page) In Auckland, over 40,000 people crowded the Eden Park Stadium where Diana took part in the Maori ritual of the rubbing noses. (Facing page) Diana, in a beautiful white hat for the visit to Manakau, on April 19, watches a fire-fighting demonstration. (Inset) On a visit to the Ayer's Rock Diana admiring the stunning view at sunset. (Previous page) In their busy itinerary the Prince and Princess of Wales visited Queensland's rural industries where they met workers at the Yandina ginger factory, and were welcomed by thousands of flag-waving children.

(Facing page) 1985. In Florence, smart and simple in a white suit with a black bow tie. (Above) Hats were Diana's trademark for a period — a nautical look and a sugary blue bowed hat for Italy. At that time even a country as fashion conscious as Italy eagerly imitated Diana's style in hats. (Right) Smart yellow and black for West Germany, in 1987, and a cute black and white hat for Portugal.

barefoot as in mosques and *ikebana* ceremonies. As if she loved a challenge, delicate situations brought out the best in her. She accepted being excluded (along with all other females) from royal gatherings in Bahrain. Without demur, she dug in with her fingers at Saudi picnics or with chopsticks in Japan. She found creative ways to echo local culture in her clothes; to pick up national emblems with her accessories and jewellery.

At the time of her marriage breakdown, Diana aimed to become a roving ambassadress for Britain. Had she lived, she would have been superb at the job. No matter how arduous the journey, how appalling the sights she encountered, Diana managed to stay calm, focused and smiling. In Pakistan, hairdresser Sam McKnight was reduced to tears. He turned back from Diana's grim walkabout among the sick and dying, only to watch the Princess smiling, kneeling and touching . . . fearless.

Diana's debut trip came later than projected. Commonwealth-tour plans halted for her first pregnancy. The same trip might have been further delayed had not the Queen – anticipating the couple's determination not to leave William – surprised tradition by agreeing that baby should go, too. William would be billeted at a farm in Australia and at Government House in New Zealand.

Thus began the longest, most difficult and important trip of Diana's career. Australia and New Zealand were salivating for a sight the woman they expected some day to be Queen Consort and the boy destined to succeed Charles. In the press party, we called the 42-day circus the "baby tour". On this trip, the world would see a future king crawl for the first time. We would also see Diana's first steps

June1983. Diana with the Canadian Prime Minister Pierre Trudeau. (top) Madrid, Spain 1985. The Royal couple with the Spanish Royal Family. (Facing page) 1983. Arriving at Lisbon on a visit to Portugal.

Visit to the Gulf, 1986. Diana in a two-piece silk suit in red and white designed by Catherine Walker. (Far right) Riyadh. An exotic luncheon in the desert at Thumanah. (Below) Qatar. After a surprise banquet for Charles' 38th birthday where Diana found she was the only female, the couple enjoyed an excursion to the desert. (Facing page) November 16, 1986, Bahrain. The Prince and Princess were entertained by the Emir at a state banquet. The dress was designed by the Emanuels and was gathered into a fan on the shoulder. The dress was complemented by the Spencer tiara.

as royal consort abroad. Australia was Diana's baptism by fire. Though she returned for two more Aussie tours, she would never experience such stress or adulation as in 1983. Over a million Australians travelled to see her. They delighted in her small-talk about William. But for much of the five weeks, Diana was frightened, exhausted and homesick.

Her friend Lord Palumbo shed light on the Princess as "a wonderful actress . . . totally irresistible". To observers, she seemed to take everything in her stride. At her first ever meet-the-press party in Alice Springs, Diana turned on the charm. I warned her she would have to press noses with New Zealand Maoris and suggested she should practice on Charles. She giggled and blushed beet-red saying: "I wouldn't want to give him such a thrill." For a marvellously unstuffy half-hour at Alice Springs, Diana was interviewed by children on outback radio. The young mum talked about William's teeth and his bath time frolics. For news people, this was a revelation: the secrets of the world's most famous baby divulged through Diana's rapport with farm kids. It was an early indication of the magic Diana had with ordinary folk. Sensing this, children tugged her dresses. One Outback girl grabbed her hand and would not leave the Princess for a whole visit.

With Diana, walkabouts became even more tactile experiences. She was kissed hundreds of times a day and did not complain. Terrified of doing the wrong thing, she somehow got everything right in the people's eyes. Diana later remembered the first tour of Australia as "make-or-break time for me . . . I learned how to be 'royal' in one week." She told Andrew Morton: "The whole world was focusing on me every day . . . I was thrown in the deep end."

Sydney was a madhouse. "My husband had never seen crowds like it and I sure as hell hadn't." At the Opera House, children hurled bouquets and Diana, standing in a convertible car, caught them mid-air. The royal press secretary Victor Chapman shook his head. "That girl has everything . . . she *is* everything." Whatever Australian outpost Charles and Diana visited in the next weeks, they returned every couple of days to see their son. "We didn't see very much of William," said Diana. "But at least we were under the same sky." As she told the Outback children: "He's got six teeth, so the next big thing is his starting to crawl. He's got the right movements but he hasn't done it yet."

This great event came in New Zealand. Princely in silk rompers, little William lurched from his mother's arms and crawled across a rug at Government House. The first royal crawlabout! Another first for Diana was her warm reception by the Maori. They sung and danced for her. A Maori schoolgirl was the first to press noses with Diana in the anticipated traditional *hongi*. Hearing of Diana's death fifteen years later, the same woman remembered feeling the softness of the Princess's skin and how she stood on Diana's foot in her nervousness. "She was a nice lady and very beautiful . . . to think, I *hongied* her."

In a more spectacular ethnic pageant, the cream of Maori manhood paddled the Prince and Princess in a huge war canoe. In the care of 80 bare-chested, tattooed warriors, the bespoke couple sat like Dresden statues.

As the tour lengthened, Diana grew gaunter. New Zealanders proclaimed her lovely, but too thin. Nevertheless, it was Diana they wanted to see, and if Charles happened to alight on their side of the street, they were tactless in their disappointment. "Diana!" they bellowed. At first Charles put on a brave face – "it

Egypt, May 1992. The Princess had been invited by the Egyptian President's wife to see for herself Mrs Mubarak's social welfare projects in Cairo. Diana in conversation with President Mubarak and (below right) at the Philae Temple.

(Below) Nigeria,1990. The Prince and Princess, free from formal engagements, were able to catch a glimpse of life in West Africa. Diana at Umnagabai where she visited a farming community.

(Facing page) Nigeria, Lagos 1990. Diana at a state banquet.

would have been far easier to have had two wives to cover both sides of the street and I could have walked down the middle directing the operation" he told an Auckland banquet. The audience tittered, but Diana hung her head. Her popularity was already a problem for Wales' teamwork. Later that year in Canada, Charles would grumble: "I'm only here to collect the flowers," as crowds cried for his wife. "I couldn't explain that I didn't ask for it," Diana said later. The couple figured things would even out once the public honeymoon with Diana was over. It never did. In the meantime, the newlyweds headed back to London with 52,000 gifts. Farewelling Auckland, Diana said she was "totally exhausted." In 42 days the new Princess of Wales had paid her dues.

The long first tour paved the way for more Wales' jaunts every year, with time off only for maternity leave. In their busiest season, the couple toured seven countries. The Princess's arrival brought epidemics of Diana-fever wherever she travelled. In Tokyo, Diana "look-alike" contests compelled Japanese women to parade in frilly blouses. At a more formal level, there were astonishing

Indonesia 1989. At the Tamrin Mini in Jakarta, Diana with girls in traditional costume. (Facing page) India, 1992. Both Charles and Diana had their foreheads daubed as part of the Tilak greeting when they arrived in the southern city of Hyderabad.

outbreaks of gallantry. Sumo wrestlers grunted extra loud when Diana was at ringside. Australian and Canadian premiers declared themselves bewitched by her eyes. Romantic gestures abounded. Spanish students laid down a cloak for Diana to tread on. A British soldier in Germany parachuted out of the sky, bounded up to the Princess and blushingly offered a red rose. The Sultan of Oman presented her with a fortune in diamonds and sapphires.

The Commonwealth was always deemed most important and for her third big tour, Diana planned a Canadian conquest later in 1983. Her hat and dress repeated the red and white of thousands of little flags as she arrived in Halifax. She was shadowed by her own pistol-toting woman bodyguard but Diana's biggest threat in Canada was of being loved to death. Days into the tour, an official no-kissing order was issued to walkabout crowds. (In an uncanny resurrection of Diana's legacy, teenage Prince William's arrival there would provoke the same mayhem in 1998.)

Pierre Trudeau called Diana "this radiant lady with the beautiful eyes." Experiencing princess-envy, neighbouring Americans poured across the border for a glimpse of Diana. Critics called her dresses old-fashioned. Undaunted, she wore a

Victorian costume, borrowed from the BBC, to a "Gay Nineties" barbecue. It was an uncomfortable taste of what Charles' great-great-great grandmother Queen Victoria endured every day. On a walkabout soon after, I heard the 22 year-old complain of the outfit: "I was glad to get out of that dress, it had whalebone from throat to waist."

Six months later, Diana showed her improved grasp of the family business with a solo trip to Norway. She was pale and nervous. We thought she was insecure without Charles. In fact, she was morning-sick. Harry was on his way and once

again, Diana's touring schedule was on hold. A baby later in 1985, Italian newspaper headlines screamed "Carlo e Diana !" This heralded a 17-day trial by pasta and *paparazzi* for the royal couple. Fanciful reportage in the local papers declared that Diana had said "I want from Charles a baby made in Italy." Immediately, the Queen's stalwart yacht *Britannia* was christened "the Love Boat," and it was claimed by the press that the royal lovebirds would be eating spaghetti with aphrodisiac sauce! Less amusing for Diana was the daily criticism by the Italian press of every garment she wore. They were incensed that she had not bought a new wardrobe for the tour; outraged that she dared to grace La Scala in an "ugly and banal" gown that she had worn *twice* before. The crowning insult was in Rome, where she wore a white suit and black bow tie, to which comics in the crowds screamed: "Waiter!" Her couturiers were not completely to blame. Ravaged by bulimia, Diana's figure did nothing for their garments.

There were magical moments at the Vatican, when the most beloved woman in the world curtsied to the most beloved man. Diana obeyed protocol to the letter for her meeting with Pope John Paul II. She wore black lace veils, a floor-length gown and black gloves. She seemed nervous, but the Pontiff quickly put her at ease, discussing her favourite subject – William and Harry. Diana said she had called them every day and was excited that they would join their parents in Venice. As if to atone for her first and only "fashion fiasco tour", Diana returned to Venice ten years later. In Jacques Azagury's little red cocktail dress, she knocked the gondoliers' socks off.

Foreign trips were also a good opportunity for the Waleses to show off their fancy footwork. Three times were Australians treated to Diana's dancing technique; two furious fox-trots in Sydney, and a jitterbug in Melbourne. The Queen once correctly observed that "one can't really dance in a tiara," but her inventive daughter-in-law got around the problem by converting a Queen Mary emerald choker into a bandeau, which stayed secure on her brow as she twirled in Sydney.

Washington DC's glitterati still talk of the time a Princess got "Saturday Night Fever". For a White House ball, First Lady Nancy Reagan gathered a dazzling array of partners, including Mikhail Baryshnikov, Neil Diamond and John Travolta. Diana favoured them all. The Russian dancer sat next to Diana at dinner and when guests started signing each other's place cards, he was too shy to ask for Diana's

autograph. "What's wrong?" she asked. "As a teenager I stood in the rain at Covent Garden when you were dancing. I desperately wanted *your* autograph!"

Mrs Reagan told John Travolta the Princess had a secret wish to dance with him. "John seemed a bit shy," Mrs Reagan recalls. "Of course, as soon as they started dancing (to music from "Grease"), everyone stepped aside and watched in awe . . . it was just the two of them and it was beautiful to behold!" His White House speech completely upstaged by floor show exhibition, Charles was less gushing. He snapped back at reporters' questions: "My wife would be an idiot if she didn't enjoy dancing with John Travolta."

The Wales' long tour of the Gulf States in 1986 tested another type of footwork. Though eclipsing her husband's popularity at home, Diana took a back seat in countries where women obey *purdah*. Conforming with Islamic custom, Diana took gowns that showed no more than her hands and face. At a university visit in Oman, she was sent to one corner to meet female students, 50 yards from where Charles chatted to the men. For Charles' 38th birthday banquet in Qatar (where the sexes do not mix socially), Diana was honoured with an invitation to join her husband and the Emir. The Princess and her lady-in-waiting were the only women among a sea of men in black robes. Saudi Arabian women have very diminished status. But for the golden-haired Princess, the Saudis turned on a picnic straight out of a Valentino movie. White Arab horses galloped among the sand dunes. Bedouin tents shaded priceless carpets as yet another prince royally hosted the visitors. Diana's silk tunic and baggy trousers pillowed in the desert breeze. Cool as minted yoghurt and no doubt recalling those far-off days at the Young England Kindergarten, she sat cross-legged on the rugs.

Pakistan, 1991. During the solo visit to Pakistan, at Noopur Shahan, Diana met with local women. On her arrival children scattered rose petals.
(Facing page) She covered her head with a gold-embroidered shawl when entering the Badshai mosque in Lahore and removed her shoes to show respect for the Muslin custom.

Dressing exotically was the fun part of the job, as the Princess showed during a brief visit to Bangkok for the King of Thailand's birthday in 1988. She anchored her hair back with fragrant flowers and wore a one-shouldered gown of gloriously clashing fuchsia and purple chiffon.

But travel was not just dressing up to rub shoulders with the rich and stinking rich. As Diana became more immersed in her charities, her overseas visits got down to the nitty-gritty. An ambition to help lepers grew from tours of Indonesia (1989) and Nigeria (1990). In both countries, Diana asked to visit clinics. She was photographed in the treatment centres, gloveless, shaking hands and hugging leper children. Thus Diana used her tours to champion hitherto unfashionable causes – in 1989 she showed the same hands-on compassion to children with AIDS in New York.

At their best, the touring Wales were a terrific boon for British industry. In 1985, Diana headed for the J.C. Penney chain store in a Virginia Mall and admired displays of British clothing. It was a calculated move; she knew the company had just bought $50 million in British goods and her approval cleared the racks in days. At worst, the tours kept a tantalised world informed as to the disintegrating state of "the fairy tale." We learned from the Portuguese sojourn in 1987 that the couple asked for separate hotel suites. (By Korea in 1992, their suites were on separate hotel floors!) Diana was adept making her point pictorially, to gain sympathy in the war of the Waleses. She contrived to upstage her husband at an Australian music school in 1988. Charles began to play 'cello but as the cameras rolled, his wife ruthlessly sat down at a piano and pounded out Rachmaninov. The press abandoned the Prince to his humiliation.

On his last visit to India as a single man, Charles had made a speech promising his fiancée a romantic trip to the Taj Mahal. So when she stood alone before the gorgeous love temple in 1992 – and again alone by the Sphinx in Egypt – her wistful smile underlined her Prince Charming's broken promises. And by the time Charles and Diana posed – together physically, but miles apart – on their dismal Korean tour, there was no play-acting in the body language. For days, they hardly made eye contact. The press had given up on romantic headlines and by then labelled them "The Glums".

It had been great while it lasted. But nearly ten years of travelling together as ambassadors for Queen and country were history. "We would have made the best team in the world," Diana told American editor Tina Brown. "I could shake hands till the cows come home. And Charles could make serious speeches. But it was not to be."

Italy, 1985. In happier times, in Milan. After their visit to Italy ended in Venice they were met by their two sons and spent a few days on the Royal Yacht *Britannia cruising* the Mediterranean. India, 1992. The Princess poses alone at the Taj Mahal, the mausoleum built in the 17th-century by Shah Jehan for his favourite wife. This picture fueled the speculation about the state of her marriage.

"Oh, do you think divorce agrees with me?"

Diana to fashion designer Arnold Scaasi, June '97

Before his marriage, Prince Charles bought Highgrove House in Tetbury as a family nest. He and landscaper Mollie Salisbury began the garden in 1982, planning it to mature in 15 years. Woefully, his marriage was over and his wife was dead by the time those tenderly talked-to flower beds reached full glory. At a polo game in 1981, less than a year after their marriage, I heard the usually poised prince yell at cameramen: "leave my bloody wife alone!" A funny adjective, I thought, to call his pregnant bride. With hindsight, his slip was clearly Freudian.

In August 1996, a decree absolute officially ended what the Archbishop of Canterbury had called the "stuff of fairy tales". By then, even romantics had agreed that fairy tales are often pretty Grimm affairs. Like most unsuccessful marriages, the problems began even before the couple said "I do". Buoyed in anticipation of the wedding of the century, Charles and Diana overlooked the danger spots in their relationship. So their honeymoon yacht sailed from the Rock of Gilbraltar inexorably toward far nastier rocks. What promised to be a great dynastic marriage – uniting the House of Windsor with one of England's

great old families – was semi-arranged. Not just by the maternal grandmothers and the Spencer clan but by the press and an adoring public. "The Action Man Prince" had been long-overdue for marriage and a virginal kindergarten teacher seemed like just the ticket. He simply followed the line of least resistance and married the girl. He told a friend: "I expect it will be the right thing in the end."

Through the Spencer's ancient royal ancestry, a king produced by the union would bring blood from every English monarch back to the ruling dynasty.

Together, yet miles apart. On that last tour in Korea, Charles and Diana hardly ever made even eye contact – physical contact was totally out.
(Facing page) An even earlier manifestation of the troubles as the Princess walks alone on a Norfolk beach during the Royal Family's traditional Christmas sojourn at Sandringham.

For the Spencers – who groomed Diana to win the approval of Charles and the Windsors – a queen-consort in the family was the crowning achievement in 500 ambitious years. No less rapt was the Garter King of Arms, commanded in 1981 to combine Charles' and the Spencer's coat of arms. On the couple's stationery, Althorp's unicorn reared with the Wales' lion. "It was lucky," an official at the Garter's office told me, "that the Spencers had such a nice coat of arms. Otherwise it might have been a real mess."

In 1992, Charles and Diana separated and, with gothic symbolism, Windsor Castle burned. The Queen called it an *annus horribilis*. To Wales watchers, who had observed Camillagate, Squidgygate, Andrew Mortongate and the awful Korean Tour, it was a real mess. In December, the Prime Minister, John Major, announced that the Prince and Princess of Wales would separate, not divorce. But in July 1996, a London courtroom clerk dispassionately read the names of 31 couples seeking decrees *nisi*. Couple number 31 was the Prince and Princess. Six weeks later, the divorce was finalised. Diana was no longer "Her Royal Highness" and people were not required to curtsy or even call her "ma'am". From third highest-ranking lady in the land she became, once more, a commoner. She was technically obliged to genuflect to her sons and to such low-ranking royals as Princess Michael of Kent. Diana took a lump sum of £17 million and £350,000 a year to run her office.

The most glamourous and public of royal marriages had produced the world's most public divorce. But any romance was over at least eight years before. For all Charles and Diana's dynastic suitability, they were a poor match – two lonely people seeking soulmates in exactly the wrong person – and this was was evident before the mists had cleared from their Scottish honeymoon. While courting, Diana had convinced herself and her intended that she could love the isolated, archaic lifestyle of the Windsors. "Next to Prince Charles, " she enthused in the engagement broadcast, "I know I can't go wrong." But she could. At first innocently, she stole his popularity and sidelined his serious endeavours with her explosive charisma. The Princess complained that she was given little advice in her job. But Charles did not plan on a career girl. For such a popular Prince of Wales, a princess was merely required to be a supportive wife and child-bearer. We thought she would bring fresh air to a stodgy monarchy. Indeed, the People's Princess totally redefined the style of a royal (she later dared to say the Windsors and the public should "walk hand-in-hand, as opposed to being so distant").

It hardly mattered that, at 21 years old, she was often "very daunted" by her public role. With spontaneity and the instinct for cheering people who most needed a boost, she magically came up trumps on her first try at anything. Her star quality grew to be a double-edged sword for the Windsors. She could knock the Queen off the front page by naively changing her hair style. The Queen was the most patient of mother-in-laws. But in her most majestic roles, it was unacceptable to be background music every time a certain young bride blinked. Charles learned to leave Diana at home if he wanted his speeches to be reported.

"We were a couple doing the same job," Diana told *Panorama's* Martin Bashir, "which is very difficult for anyone." She said she thought they were a good team: "I desperately wanted it to work; I desperately loved my husband." In her campaign to entice her husband, she enslaved a nation. In 1984, a London author earned the wrath of Charles' press office by declaring "the only man in England who is not in love with the Princess is her husband." The worst aspect of the statement was its truth. Dressmaker Jasper Conran attests to Diana's fruitless efforts. "No matter what (dress) you were making for her, the question was always 'will my husband think I am sexy in this?' Even when I was making maternity dresses for her, the question was the same. I found it very sad."

Love might have conquered all. But the careful training that disciplined Charles for kingship prevented him from showing enough affection to comfort an insecure wife. He needed his quiet, Victorian life in the country to balance a life of duty. She needed the confidence-boost of her smart city crowd. Charles had known the constraints of royal security since infancy. Diana despaired to her Highgrove housekeeper Wendy Berry: "It's like

living in a nightmarish police state." Everything she did was reported via a detective to Charles. Craving freedom, Diana gave her minders fits by motoring off into the Cotswolds alone. Unsure from the earliest days of the engagement of the relationship and of her own worth, Diana binge-ate and vomited several times a day for years. "It was a symptom of what was going on in my marriage," said Diana. "I was crying out for help but giving the wrong signals, and people were using my bulimia as a coat on a hanger – they decided that was the problem: Diana was unstable."

Devastated by the mood swings that came with the disease, Charles retreated to books and erudite chums. She stopped pretending to love the Scottish grouse moors and pottering around in the garden. When the family retreated to Balmoral, Diana found excuses to stay in London. If Charles appeared in his gardening clothes at Highgrove, she would ask: "Who is getting the benefit of your wisdom today, the sheep or the raspberry bushes?" Charles' habitual pontificating also got on her wick. Soon after Harry's birth, the father criticised (perhaps digging at his own papa, who played squash during Charles' delivery) "husbands who turn up later . . . only see a baby which might have been picked off a supermarket shelf, for all they know." Said Diana: "My husband knows so much about rearing children that I've suggested he has the next one and I'll sit back and give advice."

According to friends and the royal staff grapevine, it was routine to see the national heroine in tears. She cried with Charles and without him; on her way to jobs and on her way home. She cried so much that Charles became indifferent to her tears. Camilla Parker-Bowles lived 15 minutes from Highgrove and in the calm home of his former girlfriend, he found refuge. "There were three of us in this marriage, so it was a bit crowded," Diana said urbanely in her *Panorama* interview. But like her bulimia, Charles' attachment to Camilla was a cancer to the marriage. Diana felt everyone – her husband, their mutual friends, their staff – formed a conspiracy to support husband's infidelity. She was paranoid, distrustful, and with good reason.

Imagine the dichotomy: you are the most admired woman in the world, adored of the masses by day, and abandoned by night. People you trust lie about your husband's activities. To boot, each thing you do is observed by security or recorded by the press. You never have a private minute. You fear your children will be taken away because people call you crazy. Small wonder Diana howled at the drop of a hankie. With the disillusionment and isolation she endured, the real wonder is that she was not nightly howling at the moon.

Dedicated parents, papa and mummy did not fight in front of the boys. But rows at Highgrove were legendary. Housekeeper Wendy Berry remembers: "We would hear the sitting room door bang shut and count the steps as Diana fled to her room. A cry of 'hard hats' or 'action stations' would come from one of

The beginning and the end: a Post Office First Day cover produced for the 1981 wedding (top) and the certificate of divorce granted in 1996.

the police."

At her engagement Diana had called Charles her "tower of strength". Seven years and two sons later, the Prince took refuge in an ivory tower in Balmoral for 37 days. Diana stayed with the boys at Kensington Palace. What had been whispered subversively for years was now headlines. Charles and Diana were completely estranged. Under pressure, they reunited at Highgrove. The reconciliation was more painful than the separation. Within 24 hours, Diana roared off to London, alone.

Yet for five more years, the couple put on brave public faces and went about their duties. They toured diligently overseas. They waved from the balcony after Trooping the Colour. Soaking, they listened to Pavarotti in the rain. They sent out family Christmas cards and smiled for photo-calls with the kids. When people gossiped too loudly about their apparent lack of affection, Charles resorted to lavish displays of hand-kissing at polo matches. Generally, they tried to give the public what it expected from a royal marriage. In a monarchy that could ill-afford the scandal of divorce, Charles was determined to be king. Diana was a world-class celebrity and did not want to let her fans down. Charles had his soulmate in Camilla at Highgrove, Diana indulged secret flings with several men in London.

Staff marvelled that the Waleses could be screaming and crying at home before an engagement. When their car arrived, Diana dried her eyes and commanded "Come on, Charles, they're waiting". Off they went. Like a video plot that had been paused for a couple of hours, the row resumed the minute they got home. He was a dedicated pro, she an amazing actress. Seeing how ill Prince Andrew's wife fared in her divorce at the hands of the Windsors, Diana bided her time and learned from Sarah's misfortunes. So after the love was gone, the Wales' sad little charade continued for years.

But there was just too much ill-will to stay hidden forever. Royal observers were frequently reminded that the Wales' coexisted, not in a state of matrimony, but of truce. Anwar Hussein photographed Prince William at a birthday photo-call. Looking at his picture "overs" later, I saw he had accidentally captured the essence of the marriage– the blank-faced parents at each end of a garden bench, separated by eighteen inches of gloom. Sadly carved in the back rest between them was the family crest. Portrait of a marriage.

The togetherness act grew transparent on tour. To avoid the indignity of being snubbed when crowds howled for his wife, Charles made his speeches and walkabouts alone. Meanwhile, she posed like a tragic heroine, achingly alone at the romantic spots of the ancient world. When Charles went a kiss too far after a polo match in India, Diana effectively slapped his face by turning her head away. She was sick of the game.

The couple were skiing together in Austria when Diana heard of her father's death. She at once returned home and only at the Queen's bidding did she allow Charles to accompany her. "It's a bit late to start acting the caring husband now," she bridled. Eventually, it was the Princess who decided her

"acting career was over". In a move she later regretted, she colluded with Andrew Morton to produce *Diana: Her True Story*. The best-selling book gave a one-sided, but devastating, account of her miseries at the hands of bulimia, the royal establishment, Charles and his mistress. Avalanches of dirty linen soon piled up around Kensington Palace. An old recorded phone chat with her friend James Gilbey surfaced in the press, hinting at indiscretions and revealing feelings better left unsaid about "that f*****g family." Soon after, stories surfaced of an affair with her riding instructor, James Hewitt.

Evidently, the Queen still had hopes for the couple and insisted they make one last ambassadorial mission to Korea. They barely made eye contact for four days and even flinched when they accidentally touched. The Prime Minister announced their separation one month later.

Though it was first stated that divorce was not likely, ensuing controversies surrounding the non-marriage brought on the inevitable. Intimate taped conversations thrust the adultery of Charles and Camilla down the public throat. Against all advice, Charles allowed himself to be interviewed on television, admitting the affair. In the confessional style of the Oprah Winfrey generation, Diana aired her marital woes for her own TV interview in 1995. She also criticised the monarchy and disloyally hinted that Charles might harbour doubts about being king. This was her undoing. The Queen cried "enough!" Writing to both Charles and Diana, she urged divorce. The lawyers went to battle. By July '96, Diana was £17 million richer but, to her anguish, stripped of the HRH she considered essential to her continued public standing. It was some consolation that Prince William soothed her "I really don't mind what you are called . . . you're mummy".

"We had struggled to keep it going," Diana had said of the 15-year partnership. "But obviously we'd both run out of steam . . . I take some responsibility that our marriage went the way it did. But I won't take any more because it takes two to get in this situation. We both made mistakes." She regretted the final dissolution of the marriage as "the worst day of my life."

Despairing at the mayhem both Andrew and Charles' choice of wives had brought upon the family, the Queen had earlier betrayed a trace of black humour to one of her household. "You take in two girls from broken homes," she muttered "and this is how they repay you . . ."

While the PR battle between her and Charles raged, one of Diana's most spectacular coups was her appearance at the Serpentine Gallery (facing page) on the evening that Charles was to make his notorious adultery admission on television. The famous black "revenge dress" was commissioned from Christina Stambolian long before Diana actually wore it in public.

She brings oxygen into the room . . . most people take it out

Marguerite Littman, founder of the Aids Crisis Trust

Take a picture of HRH the Princess of Wales circa 1981. Compare it to Diana snapped in the year of her death. You have a Barbie doll who became Warrior Princess. The difference is not just age; it is also attitude. In her thirties, Diana did much more than cut her hair and lost the clutter from her clothes. Much more than style, she gained focus and power. You could hear it in her voice. When I first spoke to Diana a lifetime before, her words spurted out in a juvenile gush. By the Nineties, her public speeches were part Margaret Thatcher, part Emma Thompson. You could read the changes around her eyes. Her body screamed liberation, with at least 15 pounds more authority. She no longer needed big hair, big jewels and gowns. In parting from Charles, she also divorced the tiara and the pretence that went along with it. "My acting career is over," she had determined.

She was certainly speaking from experience when she said : "The biggest disease this world suffers from is people feeling unloved. I can give love . . . I'm very happy to do that and I want to do that." She told her friend Rosa Monckton: "I want to walk into a room, be it a hospice for the dying or a hospital for sick children, and feel that I am needed. I want to *do* not just *be*".

Sensing that the challenge would need stamina, Diana had already tackled her biggest demon. With counsellors and the doctors she dubbed "shrinks", she learned to understand bulimia. Victory came when at her most depressed – usually at Balmoral with the Windsors – she could open a refrigerator door and walk away without devouring the entire contents. (People familiar with the disorder know it is not about gluttony or vanity, but about insecurity.)

"When my bulimia finished," Diana said, "I felt so much stronger, mentally and physically, so I was able to soldier on in the world." Wellness also brought fitness. Carolan Brown, Diana's first personal trainer, said: "She worked incredibly hard at getting fit and as she got fitter, she began to realise 'yes, I am a good-looking woman and that gives me some power'. I worked on her posture, generally strengthening her torso so that she could hold her head up with confidence." Sitting for a 1995 portrait by Henry Mee, Diana did not ask for a beautiful canvas. "Make me look strong!" she told the painter.

Big is best in the Nineties. Without a husband to dwarf, Diana knew she could compete with any of the supermodels. Jimmy Choo's 3.5 inch heels took her height to over six feet. She reinvented the delicate Princess bride as an Amazon. Inevitably the inches crept back around her arms, legs and shoulders. "She often laughed about how designers commented on her dress size changing, and how she had become broader across the back," says Jenni Rivett, another personal trainer. The famous black "revenge dress" was commissioned from Christina Stambolian long before Diana actually wore it in public. At the Christie's auction where it sold for £39,000, Diana confessed to the designer: "That little black dress – I had a job to squeeze into it!" She had regained womanly curves not seen since her engagement pictures. Diana's philanthropy in selling her older gowns for charity is undoubted, but by 1997, many of them were too small and she did not care. One of her hairdressers recalls Diana's belly laugh when zipping up a favourite Jacques Azagury dress on her 36th birthday and finding it too tight in the bust. "Oh well, I'll wear my second choice," was her solution. The fashion plate was finally refusing to let clothes wear her.

The many moods of Diana show up in her love-hate relationship with the media. The *paparazzi* she detested –as did the *bona fide* press photographers who covered her activities as Princess of Wales all through the Eighties. (Above) A confident, smiling Diana strides out of the Chelsea Harbour Health Club where she took regular exercise after the separation. But (facing page) there was more often in the later years the stress and strain caused by the hounding of the *paparazzi*.

The power of Diana's landmark 1993 "bulimia speech" came after many hours tuition from London actor and voice coach, Peter Settelen. When Settelen first heard Diana speak on radio in 1992, he described her voice as "nervous and gauche, hitting all the wrong words with a very thin, little girl's voice". The teacher later told me that the old Diana "had virtually no self-confidence. She had spent years being lied to by all the people around her about the true relationship Charles had with Camilla. A wall of silence. Just like when she was a child and her father didn't talk about her mother."

Settelen – whose credits include cameos in *A Bridge too Far* and in Agatha Christie's *Poirot* TV series – improves people's speech with methods that include vocal exercises and massage. He worked at restoring Diana's confidence. "We had a deal that she would no longer bow her head, that she would stand tall. I also knew that if I could get her up in front of an audience . . . speaking more powerfully and passionately than she had ever done before, her confidence would increase by leaps and bounds. People would no longer treat her like a bimbo . . . and really start to listen to what she had to say." Ironically, when he was photographed going to lunch with his pupil, a tabloid described Settelen as "as dashing Robert Redford lookalike." Eventually, Diana's "mystery fella" played such a large part in bolstering her morale that the same girl who refused speaking parts in school plays could get up and address international luminaries like Henry Kissinger.

Diana and Settelen wrote some of her most important speeches together, including the historic "time and space" statement that announced her semi-retirement. Settelen considers Diana's previous collaboration with Andrew Morton as the only way she knew at the time to "express out" negative feelings. "I tried to get the energy out through her speeches, turning the energy that was hurting her into something powerful and positive," he says.

Diana spat words out like venom in the 1993 eating disorder speech; it was one area where she was an expert. Settelen calmed her nerves ahead of time, advising her: "Imagine you're a hooker – you've been there, done that and you're fine." After the address, Diana spotted her teacher walking on the roadside. "She stopped her car, flung open the door. Then she swung out her leg and said 'Not bad for a hooker, eh?' " On the telephone with Settelen later, she was euphoric. "I'm just so excited," she exclaimed. "I really felt as though I expressed me for the first time, really connected to the audience." Replied Settelen: "What you're feeling now is your power." The work was rewarded when her friends failed to recognise her on the telephone. "You sound so strong," marvelled Lady Elsa Bowker. "I am strong," said Diana.

Diana-power triumphed during an awkward visit to Nepal, soon after her marriage separation and the embarrassing release of taped conversations with James Gilbey. The Palace apparently asked her hosts to downgrade her reception. Unworried, Diana turned the tour into a victory. Without fanfares or red carpet (the playing of "God Save the Queen" was omitted at her welcome), she prototyped the style of no-fuss royalty, relevant to its mission. As she would risk all in 1995 for the controversial BBC TV *Panorama* interview, she toughed it out in Argentina

with more than 360 journalists. For four days, the pace was relentless. "You must be tired," a well-wisher sympathised. "I am stronger than I look," replied Diana. Serious hair styles are for women who want to be taken seriously. She earlier asked stylist Sam McKnight how to revamp fluffy, Eighties hair. He recalls: "I said, I'd get rid of it . . . we put a piece of polythene around her neck and gave her a kind of early Nineties hair cut." Still later, Diana quit perming and adopted a coiff short enough to style by running her fingers through it. With Jackie Kennedy as inspiration, she wore neater hats, fuss-free outfits and minimal jewels. Installing a sun bed in Kensington Palace, she dispensed with stockings and went bare-legged to many summer events. In itself, this was a real liberation for a woman who had once scolded a lady-in-waiting for not wearing tights!

Diana opens Leicester University's Richard Attenborough Centre for Disability and the Arts. (Facing page) Diana spent her last birthday, her 36th, attending a gala dinner at the Tate Gallery.

The June 1996 Chicago visit coincided with the final throes of her divorce battle. Determined not to let her anxiety show, she aimed to go out with a bang, not a whimper. America was just the place for bravado – you cannot feel defeated when you are dressed by Versace, serenaded by Tony ("Smile-Though-Your-Heart-is-Breaking") Bennett, cheered by thousands – and when people pay over £1 million to charities just to dine near you. "That trip," says Sam McKnight, "was a pinnacle for her. She was so buoyed up with confidence . . . she looked amazing. She had found her true self and it was a big change for her."

Marguerite Littman, founder of the Aids Crisis Trust, summed up the New Age Diana in 1997: "She's more sure-footed now, very disciplined. She exercises. She gets up early. She's sensible but it's not a boring sensible . . . she brings oxygen into the room – most people take it out." How she had grown by then . . . and that learning curve included her curious love-hate affair with the world's media.

When the first foreign *paparazzo* came to London, desperately seeking Diana, I remember it well. It was 1982 and Diana was pregnant. The world

was acting like no one ever had a baby before. The Parisian picture man told me photographers snapped every step Princess Caroline of Monaco took. So his agency was amazed that the royal English star still had unfilmed moments; that namby-pamby London pressmen consulted court circulars or polo club schedules for photo-ops. Huge sums of money went unearned every time Diana went shopping. This was about to change.

The *paparazzo* took a West End hotel room and worked as no royal photographer had even considered. Early morning, he took his post outside Kensington Palace, a small car at the ready. Whenever Diana left home, he followed. Before long, newspapers all over the world printed "snatch"pictures of a Princess in what had once been her private life. The lone lensman at the Palace was joined by dozens, foreign and local. They brought walkie-talkies and motor bikes into the hunt.

It is pointless to argue whether the press created or simply fed the voracious international addiction to Diana; the fact was, she sold papers better than naked Page-Three girls. Editors were soon unsatisfied by posed photos from her official engagements. They wanted her shopping, exercising, driving. If she went on holiday, they showed the world a Princess in a bikini. If William made pee-pee in a flower bed, it was front-page. If Diana brushed hands with a man-friend – blimey! stop the presses!

Prices and risks grew greater. The only pictures of Diana riding with her mother-in-law were snapped after the Parisian trespassed at Sandringham. In his accented English, he told me how hilarious it was. The Queen had scowled: "You're very rude!" Such a reprimand would have cut me to the soul. To the Queen, it was an outrageous experience. Diana had simply hung her head. No audacity surprised her now.

She grew more vocal in later years, screaming at the *paparazzi* who then hunted her in packs: "You make my life hell!" Colour pictures of her, spread-eagled on a leg-press machine at her gym, were the last straw for Diana. She retired from public life, believing she might regain "time and space". If anything, she declared open-season on herself. The resulting paucity of pictures turned Diana-sightings into feeding frenzies. She considered *paparazzi* strikes as physical assaults from which – having deliberately shed her police protection – she had no shield. In tears, she told her hairdresser about motorbike lensmen who dogged her at traffic lights, calling four-letter insults to snap her response. "She felt she had been raped daily," said Sam McKnight. "No wonder she had black moments."

As a royal fiancée, she had stepped uncomfortably before the motor-driven flashlights. "I was very daunted," she said on television, "because, as far

(Above) June, 1996. A gala dinner in Chicago, and (facing page) a cuddle for a child during a visit to the city's Cook County Hospital. After her separation and subsequent divorce Diana's popularity in the USA, far from falling, reached new heights.

as I was concerned, I was a fat, chubby 20-year-old and I couldn't understand the level of interest." She believed it was because her Prince was so well loved. She was also told (as Palace press secretary Michael Shea also told me in 1981), that the Queen expected things to quieten down on the Diana front "in a year or so". Greater foresight came from Princess Grace of Monaco. She took the trembling 20 year-old aside at her first engagement and advised "Don't worry, it'll get worse . . ."

It did. But through a mixture of savvy and innocence, the ingenue perfected her press act with amazing speed. Always, there were *paparazzi* who were simply beyond the pale. But with her legitimate press regulars, Diana developed a symbiotic relationship enduring the length of her front-page reign. They might manipulate her. She was embarrassed, for example, when they contrived a Princess-bountiful scenario in Zimbabwe (Diana had to dish out rice; this, she felt, demeaned Africans). But she could be equally manipulative if a picture conveniently pushed her wagon. Neither did she hesitate in grabbing front pages for points as the Waleses battled for public approval. Weeks before her death – and a day after berating newsmen for snapping her at St Tropez – Diana gambolled happily in her swimsuit, aware that lenses

In her last, few hectic months, Diana showed no sign of lessening her commitment to charity work. (Above) July, 1997. At Northwick Park Children's Centre in Harrow, London. (Facing page). Attending a press reception for the auction of some of her dresses at Christie's, New York.

captured every pose. She knew something photographers did not. That her lovely body in tomorrow's papers would ruin Camilla Parker-Bowles' 50th birthday . . .

Diana's press gambit was a confusing succession of that love-hate. One day she might want to abandon public life and be left alone. The next day she might leak her movements to ensure coverage of good works. Then she colluded with a favourite tabloid reporter or co-operated in a tell-all book. Like many megastars, she wanted to decide what was printable and what was private. Her friend Lord Palumbo describes the ploy: "She wanted them (the media) on her own terms – to use the press when she wanted . . ."

It is cruel to both Princess and to papers to say, that as she lived by the press, she died by it. Still, neither party's treatment of each other was pristine. An official inquest exonerated those *paparazzi* – who pursued Diana's car and photographed her dying – from actually causing the accident. But drunken chauffeur or not, the al-Fayed Mercedes would not have sped so

dangerously if its passengers were not at their wits' end over unwanted photography. In the days following Charles Spencer's "blood on their hands" statement, those *paparazzi* who daily made her cry in the streets were rightly attacked. One hopes such people with Diana's tears, if not her blood, on their hands – may never have a decent night's sleep again. But unjustly, legitimate news people were also tarred by Lord Spencer's sweeping brush stroke.

He forgot the cosy relationship Diana sustained with her steady press entourage. Never quite friends, they were certainly not enemies. She certainly identified with the women in her entourage. At last conquering her nail-biting habit, Diana proudly teased Jayne Fincher – a photographer who still nail-nibbles – "haven't you grown 'em yet?" Jayne told the Princess of crying after missing pictures of Diana and baby William leaving Paddington St Mary's Hospital after delivery in 1982. "Well, I was crying, too," commiserated Diana. "Coming down those stairs was so painful." She was younger than all of us but she could be motherly; sometimes scolding, sometimes solicitous. She wagged her finger at tabloid writer James Whitaker for disclosing that she wore thermal underwear. "I have visions of you lying on the street looking up my dress!" she said at the next meet-the-press event. When sharing a flight with her press corp, she sent a bottle of

champagne back to a writer who was flavour-of-the-month. Photographers entered Diana's good books by sending her prints of particularly flattering shots. She always thanked them.

At her press conference in Egypt, photographer Anwar Hussein told Diana bartenders would not serve him because he was a Moslem. She at once disappeared into the kitchen and returned with a glass of wine for him. Like many of her long-serving press pack, Hussein was devastated by Diana's death. "Over the years I had probably seen her more than my own children – it was terrible, like losing someone in my family." Another familiar photographer, who many times snapped her in unauthorised situations, requested an item for a celebrity auction at his church. She declined, but wrote a personal cheque for £300.

Diana was called a media creation and it cannot be argued that she rose to superstardom via press glorification. In turn, newspapers often adopted a parental responsibility in chiding the sometimes-naughty child they had raised. Diana wept over it. She told author Anthony Holden she could never enjoy her weekend "until I know that someone else is on the front page of the *News Of the World*". But throughout sixteen years of fame, hers were not the actions of a woman

Meet the press: when Diana, now separated from the Prince of Wales, visited Argentina in 1996, this was the press pack that greeted her on her arrival in Buenos Aires. (Facing page) June, 1997. At the Shri Swaminarayan Mandir in Neasden, London, mere weeks before her death.

who hated publicity. She loathed the *paparazzi* who hunted her in packs. She mostly courted the legitimate press. Through this strange relationship, she was doomed to be centre-stage of a global soap opera and only tragedy could end the season. Diana's death blurred the lines between fantasy and reality. In South Africa, Charles Spencer broke the news to his twin daughters. "I've got some awful news," he began. "I'm afraid Auntie Diana has been killed." One twin smiled and said: "But not in real life, daddy."

In her philosophical moments Diana probably accepted, as even the most conservative papers did, that the phenomenon of her celebrity could not distinguish which part of her life was public interest and which was not. Body and soul, she belonged to the world.

You cannot comfort the afflicted without afflicting the comfortable

Words written by Diana on a card she kept on her desk

One of Diana's favourite photographs taken by Anwar Hussein when the Princess visited a charity cancer hospital in Lahore. Diana was deeply moved as she cuddled a child who had been blinded by a brain tumour. "I don't know why," said Diana, "but I knew he was going to die . . . I hugged him very tight. I can remember his face, his suffering, his voice. I haven't forgotten."

We were on the border between Mozambique and Zimbabwe," remembers the Reverend Tony Lloyd, Director of the Leprosy Mission. "There were streams of refugees coming over the hills. Diana spotted a woman leper too weak or faint to join the rest. I hadn't, and I was the expert. She went to help . . . there were no photographers, but it was a beautiful sight, Diana holding this woman's stump where once a hand had been, in both her beautiful hands." Diana found a motto for a new life. "You cannot comfort the afflicted without afflicting the comfortable." She wrote the words on a piece of card and propped them against a statue of Jesus on her desk.

With insight she had gained from turning her own life around in the early 1990s, Diana became very serious about helping others. Cover-girl humanitarianism invited cynicism but Diana had found an extraordinary ally in

Mother Theresa of Calcutta. "You know, you could not do my work and I could not do yours," the nun told her. "We are both working for God." Both women died within days of each other in 1997.

In her efforts for the afflicted, Diana supported scores of causes. These included drug dependency clinics, marriage guidance centres and shelters for abused women and children. During tours of Indonesia and Nigeria, she arranged to visit lepers. "She was hugely compassionate," said the Rev. Lloyd of his patron. "Perhaps because she suffered so much rejection herself . . . she had an empathy for lepers who were cast out of their families." It is no coincidence that Diana' death was greatly mourned by the gay community: her tenderness for AIDS sufferers did more for social acceptance of the disease than that of any philanthropist. "No one in this country has ever done anything so symbolic for us," said a hospital official in New York after Diana was pictured cuddling a child with AIDS in 1985. One of her most powerful speeches touched this very issue. She said: "HIV does not make people dangerous to know, so you can shake their hands and give them a hug – heaven knows, they need it. What's more, you can share their homes, their work places and their playgrounds and toys."

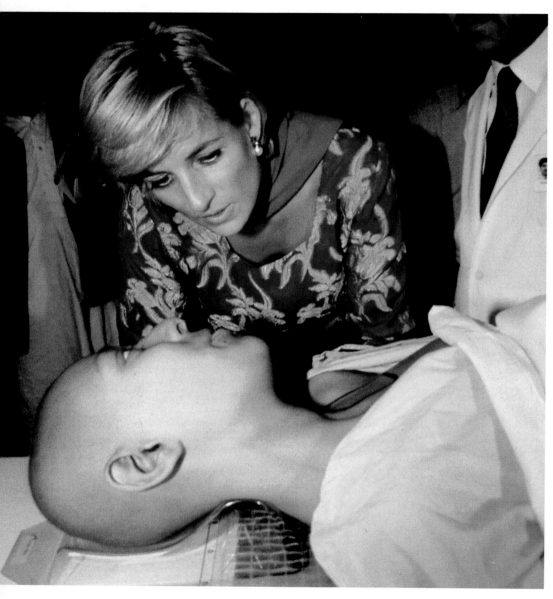

Diana said: "It's amazing. All people want to be touched . . . if you just reach out your hand and let them touch you, the impact is extraordinary." Professor Michael Adler, Chairman of the National AIDS Trust, remembers Diana's warmth. "She was at her most relaxed – radiant – and she left behind a radiance. If you went back to the ward after her visit, people were on the ceiling!"

In her own intuitive way Diana had stumbled upon the greatest healing tool of all. Even she was staggered by her power. She told her friend Lord Putnam: "It's amazing. All people want to be touched . . . if you just reach out your hand and let them touch you, the impact is extraordinary." Professor Michael Adler, Chairman of the National AIDS Trust, remembers Diana's warmth. "She was at her best (with patients) she was her most relaxed – radiant – and she left behind a radiance. If you went back to the ward after her visit, people were on the ceiling!" In the five months before he died of AIDS, art dealer Adrian Ward-Jackson was visited regularly by the Princess. She also

brought her sons to his bedside so they could learn about the disease and about the art of comforting. Such visits exhausted her – she would return home to cry for hours – but Diana was enriched by the work.

Professor Adler feels she identified with stigma-disease sufferers because of her own damaged upbringing and unhappy married life. "She felt she hadn't had the sympathy she should have had. She felt she could repair that by her work with groups who were marginalised." After helping to nurse Adrian Ward-Jackson, Diana wrote: "I reached a depth inside that I never imagined was possible." She did not find hospice visits or working with the terminally ill a chore, Peter Settelen told me. "We often talked about death, she was not afraid of it. She said how easy she found it to be with people who were dying – of looking death in the face."

On a personal level, she was always there for sick friends. Liz Tilberis actually credits Diana with healing powers that helped the fashion editor survive her cancer bout. More than just buying dozens of dresses from Catherine Walker, Diana also visited and counselled the designer who was recovering from breast cancer. As a special boost, the Princess sent a very public "get-well" by wearing a white lace Walker gown for a Breast Cancer fund raiser in America. Her outfits spoke of her compassion in other practical ways. When visiting the blind, she carefully chose to wear fabrics with interesting textures – such as velvet – so she would be more interesting to the touch. Though dozens of pairs of kid gloves were delivered to the Princess for her trousseau, she did not think them touch-friendly, and never wore them.

Compassion did not guarantee more humane treatment for Diana, however. By 1993, press intrusion in her private life had become unbearable. Using her new speaking skill with headline-making effect, she announced a withdrawal from public life. She did not intend to drop her good works, just to intensify them in more restricted areas. Diana knew her patronage was a godsend for causes with low public acceptance. So lepers, AIDS sufferers and the homeless kept their patron Princess. She also pledged help for cancer patients through the Royal Marsden Hospital and London's Great Ormond Street Hospital for Children. Culturally, Diana's aid for the English National Ballet championed a childhood passion she never outgrew.

Good as her word, she wrote personal cheques for these charities. She loaned her face to ballet posters and was trotted out at glittering charity galas. As she intended, her physical presence at any event sent donations through the roof, particularly in America. On a trip that raised $US 1.4 million for cancer causes, high-rollers in Chicago forked out big-time to sit near the beautiful Princess. Singer Tony Bennett remembers Diana's look of disbelief when encountering a standing ovation – "She gave me a quick look like, 'what's going on here?' ₒ because I don't think she ever saw such an outpouring of love."

Diana's most brilliant charity ploy was in 1997, when Prince William suggested she auction off 79 of her most famous evening gowns. She threw herself into every stage of planning for her "Sequins Saves Lives", even posing in the gowns for catalogue pictures. Held just three months before her death, the sale was the biggest charity auction ever staged at Christie's, New York. Bidders came from all over the world, raising over $US 3.25 million for AIDS and cancer charities. Every gown sold. The velvet "John Travolta" gown greased away for a bid of $222,500.

Before and after her death, the Princess had a greater effect on charity than any other person in the 20th century. "Diana used her power like a magic wand, waving it in all kinds of places where there was hurt," said Debbie Tate, who works with abused and HIV-positive children in Washington DC. "And everywhere she used it, there were changes – almost like a fairy tale." Old friends such as Imran and Jemima Khan in Pakistan could also call on Diana. One of her favourite pictures of herself was taken by photographer Anwar Hussein in Khan's charity cancer hospital, Lahore. Diana was deeply moved as she cuddled a child who had been blinded by a brain tumour. "I don't know why," said Diana, "but I knew he was going to die . . . I hugged him very tight. I can remember his face, his suffering, his voice. I haven't forgotten." Anwar Hussein recalls the incident: "The little boy was blind. But he turned his face up like he could see her. He seemed to draw amazing energy from her face . . . Diana rocked him with her eyes closed, like she was praying or trying very hard to take some of his pain away."

In her last years, Diana described her causes as "a good and essential part of my life. A kind of destiny." Written on her memorial shrine at Althorp are her own passionate words: "Whoever is in distress can call me. I will come running wherever they are."

Perhaps sensing that she had little time left, she wanted her commitment to be of real – and not just visual – value. Lord Deedes, the veteran journalist-cum-politician who travelled in Bosnia with the Princess, marvelled at her stamina in allowing 30 minutes for each injured person she met. This meant 15-hour days. "These gestures were not an act designed for the cameras nor designed to show how compassionate she was," said Lord Deedes. "She was doing these things without anybody watching. It was genuine . . . instinctive."

Nevertheless, Diana could not begrudge the sheer cosmetic ability of a Princess to lure money from pockets. Relate, a marriage guidance organisation, was strapped to raise £9,000 a year before she became patron. With Diana as figurehead in 1989, fund raising jumped to nearly £240,000. It was yet another cause Diana espoused through personal motivation. A speech she made to the group hinted at her own shattering experiences: "I have seen the tears, the anguish, the raw emotion, hurt and pain caused by the split between couples," she said.

A woman finding a new role in her life – Diana in the minefields of Angola and (facing page) with some of the innocent victims of the millions of landmines scattered throughout that war-torn country. She also visited Bosnia – her last trip before her death – where the horrors she saw only served for her to double her efforts for a worldwide ban. Her campaign to have landmines abolished was hooted at by MPs in Britain's then-Conservative Government, but when it was replaced in May 1997 by a Labour Government they immediately put their shoulder to the wheel and the result was moves to have a worldwide ban.

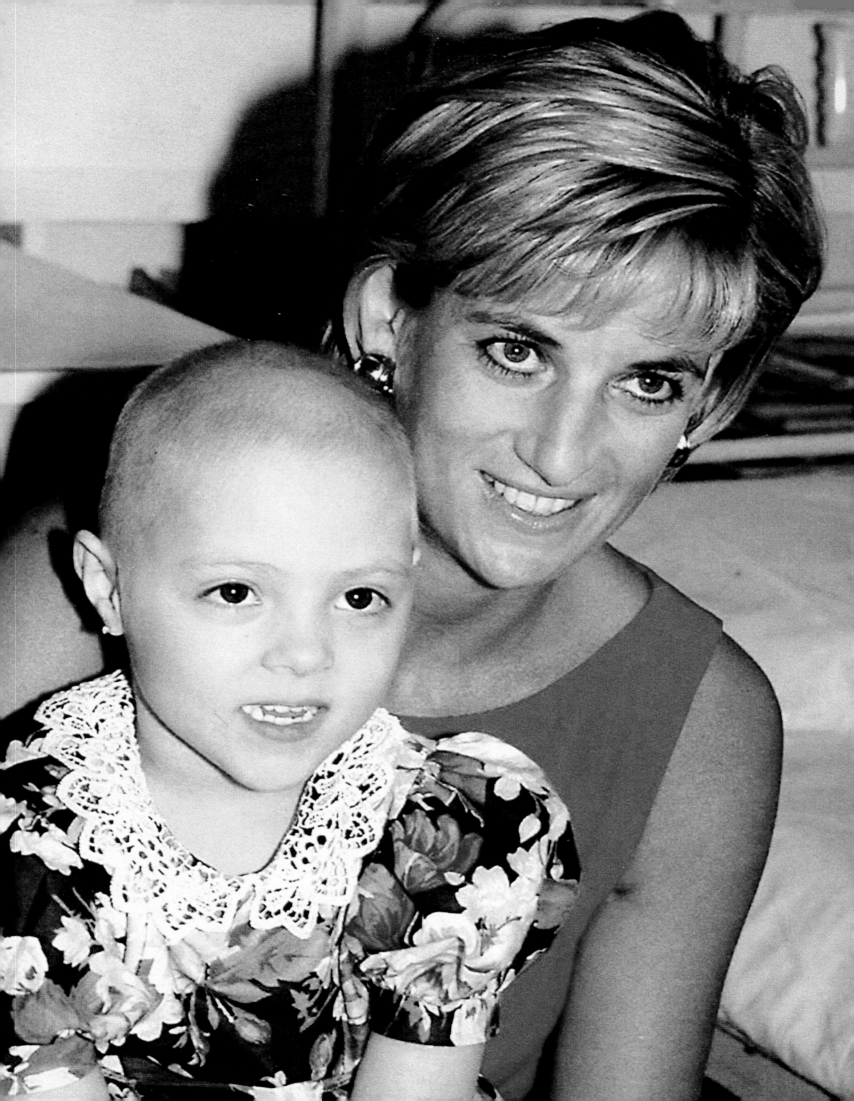

Diana literally ran into minefields for her final campaign. As British vice-president of Red Cross, she lobbied outspokenly to ban landmines. Predictably, the decision to act came straight from her heart. "A lot of information started landing on my desk," she said. "The pictures were so horrific . . ." Diana decided to raise world consciousness of the issue and spurned criticism by the then Tory Government that she was meddling politically. "What's to discuss," she demanded, "when people are being blown up?" In Angola and Bosnia, she trailed her inevitable press party as allies. "I hope," she told them, "that by working together we shall focus world attention on this vital – but until now, largely neglected – issue." Sure enough, shots of the glamourous activist in minefields garnered world press. No one drew attention to an issue like Diana. Her old friend Lady Elsa Bowker asked Diana if she were not afraid for her own safety. "I'm never afraid when I'm doing good," replied Diana.

Pictured in Armani jeans with legless children, Diana roused sneers from some Tory Party members. She was called a "loose cannon". Her response was defiant. "I am not a political figure, nor do I want to be one . . . I come with my heart . . . I'm a humanitarian figure. I always have been and I always will be." Spurred by her efforts and by the global appreciation for Diana after her death, 120 countries signed an anti-landmine treaty in 1997. This might not have happened without the compelling pictures from Diana's crusades to Angola and Bosnia – pictures that would never have graced the popular press had not a princess been centre-frame. She had waved her magic wand and even after she lay in her grave, the changes still came.

It perhaps reflects on the saintliness Diana attained for some that the figure 36 – her age at death – took on a mystical significance for many people donating to her memorial fund. Many children gave 36 pence. A more common gift was £36. A few donations of £36,000 came in. Thus about £1 million a week poured into the Diana, Princess of Wales Memorial Fund for much of 1998. Though beset with administrative rifts and embarrassingly slow at first to dispense money, the fund was predicted to raise £100 million before the end of 1998.

"She had been so worried", wrote her friend Liz Tilberis, "particularly when her HRH title was taken away, that she wouldn't be able to maintain the kind of stature that she had begun to achieve within the charity world. She was afraid she had lost it all. But in death, it was clear that she had really won it all."

"Just tell me, is it bliss?"
"Yes, bliss . . . 'bye"

Diana's final telephone conversation with Rosa Monckton, August 27 1997

People think at the end of the day, a man is the only answer." the royal divorcée once said. "Actually, a fulfilling job is better for me." By that stage, every time she had loved – James Hewitt, Oliver Hoare and James Gilbey – she embraced huge scandals. Her flirtation with Rugby hero Will Carling helped destroy his marriage. A crush on Hasnat Khan was too hot for the publicity-shy cardiologist to handle. She told friends she hoped to remarry. "But who would take me on?" she sighed. By summer of 1997, to use a chilling metaphor, there seemed to be light at the end of the tunnel. Diana had the fulfilling job. She was a successful charity spearhead and humanitarian activist. Britain's new Prime Minister, Tony Blair, promised a roving ambassadress role.

And, as the Mediterranean basked in August sunshine, it seemed Diana at last had her man. Five days before her death, she telephoned her confidante Lady Elsa Bowker and claimed: "I have never been so happy as I am now. I have never been so spoilt . . . so taken care of . . . all the things that I never had." Diana was enjoying yet another cruise, alone with her new lover. Finally, she had a man who was young, single and adored the deck she walked on. For once, she did not care if the world knew. Complete with colour pictures, the romance was headlines everywhere. During the sun-filled days in the south of France, she had little vacation from the press. Peeved at the attention when William and Harry were with her, she had promised a flotilla of lensmen they would very soon "be

surprised with the next thing I do". Was Diana ready to marry Dodi al-Fayed and to live in Paris? This would indeed have surprised the media and the establishment, had not another Paris event first galvanised the planet. But the press had lately found her full of surprises. Taking her sons on holiday in St Moritz with the controversial Mohamed al-Fayed arched establishment eyebrows enough; but the speed at which her final romance hatched was the biggest fascination. London gossips were still stewing over Dr Khan when – blimey! hold the front page! – Diana was up to her chin in the Med with a man who had dated Julia Roberts.

Though the Princess and the Egyptian film producer seemed like the odd couple at first, they had had bags in common. Incredible wealth; unhappy childhoods; failed marriages; failed flings; expensive habits and the need to always watch their backs. Up until two weeks before her death, Diana professed to be in no hurry to re-marry, claiming: "I haven't taken such a long time to get out of a bad marriage to get into another one." Mid-romance, she told friends that any ring Dodi gave her would go straight on "the third finger of my *right* hand." To a Princess, comforts of the al-Fayed lifestyle were not especially seductive. But she wanted a daughter. She also needed protection from the scary circus of post-royal life in London.

Living her last months at breakneck pace, Diana worked hard and played hard. She flitted from country to country, from vocation to vacation, like a jet-setter on speed. The rate at which the Dodi affair had blossomed – she gave him her father's cherished cuff links five weeks after first holding hands at St Tropez – was dizzying. Very powerful and ambitious cupids were again orchestrating Diana's love life. It was seventeen years since the Queen Mother had conspired with Diana's grandmother, Lady Fermoy, lending her Scottish house as a refuge for Charles to go wooing. In 1997, stepmother Raine (who sat on the Fayeds' board at Harrods International) encouraged Diana to vacation with the Egyptian family.

The Princess was vigorously courted. Not just by handsome 41 year-old Dodi, either. The patriarch bought the $32 million yacht *Jonikal* only when he knew Diana was likely to come to the family compound. Very soon, the love boat would prove a sound investment in helping the son advance his suit. Mohamed al-Fayed also loaned planes, helicopters and hotel suites for Diana's travels. He is said to have promised the Windsor mansion in Paris for the lovebirds. Probably, he wanted Diana as a daughter-in-law as much as Dodi wanted her for a wife. According to intimates, Dodi was in love and hardly needed urging. "I didn't know that life could be so wonderful," he told his press agent Pat Kingsley.

And Diana? She acted cool back in London. But as in so many areas of her life, she was torn between prudence and impulse. Friends advised caution. But friends knew she was apt to ask advice and ignore it. Rosa Monckton had advised her against the first St Tropez jaunt with the al-Fayeds. Diana went anyway. Dodi had joined the family late in the vacation and the chemistry between him and Diana exploded. Returning to Kensington Palace, the Princess found pink roses from her new admirer. Days later, he swept her away in the Harrods helicopter. They weekended in Paris, completely unobserved. By the following Thursday, they were again on board the al-Fayed yacht in Nice. No photographer was snapping as they docked in Monte Carlo and ordered a diamond ring from jeweller Alberto Repossi. (The jeweller would customise the ring for collection in Paris on August 30; this was the major reason the couple returned so fatally to the Ritz.) But their vacation from publicity was almost over. By a historic *paparazzi*

Was she in love? Had he proposed? Had she accepted? Those questions will never be satisfactorily answered and have already divided the world into those who say they were to be married and those who maintain that Diana regarded it as no more than a summer fling. But of one thing there can be no doubt – the pictures of Diana and Dodi taken on that last holiday (facing page and previous page) show her glowing in a way that we hadn't seen for more than a decade. The fact that Dodi's father Mohamed, despite being the owner of that great British institution, Harrods, was a controversial figure in the British business world has cast a shadow over his version of events – a confrontation with Diana's mother when they were both in Paris to be questioned by the French examining magistrate didn't help his case either.

Diana **201** *an English rose*

coup, the first pictures of Diana embracing a lover had been quietly taken the day before, as the couple swam and lazed off Sardinia. By the time these were published, Diana was back in London with a radiance which lit her face all through her harrowing visit to Bosnia. She was completely besotted. But the fair Princess saw her suitor's faults. According to Rosa Monckton, Diana winced when Dodi detailed presents he had bought her. "That's not what I want, Rosa," said Diana. "I don't want to be bought. I have everything I want. I just want someone to be there for me, to make me feel safe and secure."

He could certainly turn her knees to jelly. When Dodi left a message on her Palace answering machine, Diana replayed it so a friend could "hear his wonderful voice". Back in the Harrods helicopter, Diana sped Dodi to Derbyshire to see her psychic, Rita Rogers. Considering Diana often saw mediums and astrologers, it seems natural that her death was widely foreseen. Several such premonitions even went on record before August 31. A British churchwoman had a vision of a huge change in society that followed "the laying down of flowers" all over the nation. She told her church about the vision before Diana died. It was afterwards called "the Diana Prophecy." On March 12, an astrologer called Marcus Hayward predicted the House of Windsor would experience "the most important event in recent royal history – a person of common birth . . . will be involved in a grave hunting incident." On August 27th, Welsh psychic Edward Williams saw Diana's distraught face in a vision. He went to his local police station and warned that Princess Diana was in great danger and was going to die. Because he had previously foretold assassination attempts on the Pope and Ronald Reagan, the police took him seriously and logged a report. A few days earlier, London clairvoyant Betty Palko (whom Diana saw regularly in the early Nineties) gave an interview to an Australian magazine. Asked if she foresaw marriage between the Princess and Dodi, she said "No". She saw death, involving a car. Palko also claimed she was visited by Earl "Johnny" Spencer's spirit. The Earl beseeched the clairvoyant to tell his daughter "to stop playing silly buggers." He concluded sadly that the Diana-Dodi affair would be all over by September, anyway.

Elton John's powerful image of a candle in the wind recalls an omen noted during Prince William's christening. The Archbishop of Canterbury held a lighted candle, which a sudden gust of wind almost extinguished. But the flame at last endured and a witness, William's godfather Sir Laurens van der Post, soon recorded the symbolism. He interpreted it as a grave crisis during William's life. The flame's revival nevertheless suggested that the Prince – and possibly also the monarchy – would survive the test.

After the August 31 tragedy, Rita Rogers claimed she had warned Dodi of a car chase in a Paris tunnel. But she was at a loss to explain why she had not seen Diana in the scenario. "She had found her soulmate," said the psychic. "And she was so happy . . ."

Natalie Symons, who styled Diana's hair at Kensington Palace, kept a diary of the last two months of her service. "Since Dodi came into her life," she wrote, " (Diana) spends more time worrying about the way she looks." By mid-August, the stylist commented: "He is the only topic of (Diana's) conversation these days. Since he came into her life, I have been called on to do a lot more evening work." August 22, the diary entry reads: "Diana and Dodi are leaving on another holiday in the Mediterranean . . . usually she is very lonely when her sons go to Balmoral . . . this summer is so different. She is glowing with happiness."

For the third time in six weeks, Diana and Dodi jetted to the south of France. The al-Fayed yacht *Jonikal* again weighed anchor. As they cruised around Sardinia, Dodi

"People think at the end of the day, a man is the only answer," the royal divorcée once said. "Actually, a fulfilling job is better for me." "She had found her soulmate and she was so happy," psychic Rita Rogers declared after Diana had taken Dodi to Derbyshire to meet her. The pictures (facing page) of the Princess on holiday with the al-Fayeds seem to back up that observation. "I have never been so happy as I am now. I have never been so spoilt . . . so taken care of . . . all the things that I never had," Diana told another confidante, Lady Elsa Bowker. There was no doubt that the romance had blossomed at breakneck speed. Perhaps that's what prompted her brother Charles to later thank God "for taking Diana at her most beautiful and radiant and when she had joy in her private life".

spoke to Pat Kingsley in Los Angeles. He said he had "great news" for the press agent. "I'm not going to tell you about it until I get to California but . . . I think you'll be thrilled for me." It is immense consolation to everyone who loved and empathised with the Princess that Diana ended her mercurial history "glowing with happiness". Charles Spencer would later thank God "for taking Diana at her most beautiful and radiant and when she had joy in her private life".

On their last day alive, the lovers gave the strongest hint that the future involved living together. Arriving in France, they drove to the home of the late Duke and Duchess of Windsor, which Mohamed al-Fayed leases from the city of Paris. Diana and Dodi spent two hours with an interior designer, examining every room of the Villa Windsor. Gregorio Martin, who tends the villa for the family, said the couple were affectionate and happy, "talking about their plans for the future. They looked at everything in the house: the boiler, every cupboard, the Princess even opened the 'fridge door to look inside. She had a detailed interest in everything . . . asking about rooms for the staff and security," said Martin.

A short time later, from the Hotel Ritz, Diana telephoned London and talked to her reporter friend, Richard Kay. Sounding happier than he had ever heard her before, she told Kay of her plans to "radically change" her style by retiring from public life in November. Before dinner, Dodi hurried off alone to the Repossi jewellery store to collect the diamond ring Diana had chosen in Monaco. In the first floor Ritz restaurant, the two dined on fish. There were roses and carnations on the table. We may never know know whether Dodi produced the ring that night, or which finger she put it on.

At 12.24 a.m., speeding to elude *paparazzi* after dinner, the couple's car crashed into the 13th concrete pillar of the Alma Tunnel. Dodi and his driver were killed at once; Diana died in hospital. Days after the fatal crash, singer Luciano Pavarotti voiced the question that is likely to haunt us forever. "I don't understand what they were doing running away," he said. "I will never understand it. Whoever goes to eat in the centre of Paris expects to be seen . . . there is no room in my head for an explanation of why they were going at that speed, unless they thought they were going to be kidnapped . . ."

Even watching for the twentieth time the video frames of Diana's exit from the Ritz, logic abandons me. As the film rolls, I feel that this time, the tragedy can be averted. After all, here she is – all cheekbones and vulnerability – *alive*. Harshly lit, she turns the revolving door and there is that wonderful energetic stride I saw leave dozens of hotels. She still has four minutes to live. If someone could just stop her this time . . . or at least tell her how much she was loved . . .

The mood of the world is different . . .

Richard Branson of Virgin Records, September 1997

Leaving Los Angeles before the funeral, I squinted into the clear California sky. A small aircraft was drawing a huge heart above the famous Hollywood sign. The sky-writer scrawled the letters "D" and "I" inside the heart. It all hung together for less than a minute before errant winds puffed the message away. It was symbolic in several ways. That without appearing in a film or even visiting Hollywood, Diana was queen in the eyes of this town. More simply, that she was in Heaven, which was somewhere above the Hollywood Hills. And more generally, that life is fragile and can be puffed away as capriciously as clouds on a September day.

At the other end of the journey, London lay under a blue sky,

Her sons, her brother, her
ex-husband and former father-in-
law bow their heads as Diana's
coffin is borne into Westminster
Abbey. The streets surrounding
the Abbey (right) were covered in
tributes to the Princess from
many of the thousands who had
camped out overnight for her
funeral.
(Facing page) The scene inside
the Abbey.

Diana **206** *an English rose*

Uncle Charles Spencer shepherds the Princes William and Harry through the people's floral tributes to their mother as they make their way to the Abbey for the funeral service. (Left) Charles and his sons are overwhelmed as they visit Kensington Palace which was inundated with bouquets as the nation showed its love for Diana.

smelling like no other city on earth. Approaching Diana's London home, Kensington High Street was a sea of whispering people, moving in one direction. They overflowed the pavements and onto the streets, stopping traffic like a silent revolution. The nearer to Diana's home, the more ominous the silence. Even the birdsong in Hyde Park seemed silenced. At the heart of the pilgrimage, Kensington Palace had become a massive shrine, festooned in up to five feet of bouquets and giving out a heady wall of perfume for miles. Diana's friend Rosa Monckton had visited the coffin in St James's following its journey home from Paris. Afterwards, she walked among the flowers at Kensington Gardens. "I could almost hear her (Diana's) voice, 'Rosa, no, not all this! For me?' For she never knew how much she was loved," wrote Rosa.

From the first bouquets poked into the Palace rails on Sunday morning when people learned of Diana's death, the floral perimeter grew daily. By Friday night, the mass formed a huge cross extending more than halfway to Kensington High Street and, in its midst, tree limbs sagged under banners and tributes. Pagan-like shrines sprung up at their trunks and at night candles lit the branches like Christmas trees. Weeks after the funeral, people still brought flowers. Before the river of decaying foliage was eventually cleared, about a million bouquets lay before the gates to Diana's home.

Almost a year later, I returned to the gilded railings every morning for a week. Each day, at least ten fresh bouquets had appeared. A police officer on duty

told me the Palace "is certainly not the same place without Diana. Sometimes I look at the front entrance to the Palace and think, I'll never see her come out of there again."

During the heady mourning week, every bouquet carried a message and it seemed that everyone in England was a poet. Taped to a railing, one read:

> That beautiful face
> and all the good things you done
> in this world
> How can we ever forget you?
> You was my Queen.

For days before the funeral, people slept in the streets just as they had for Diana's wedding. At night, thousands of candles glowed. Back in 1981, she had exclaimed on her wedding morning: "This is an amazingly big fuss for the wedding of one girl." In 1997, with a million people in the streets for her last parade, Diana had been dressed in a Catherine Walker dress and was perfectly made-up. But she would never wake to see the biggest influx of people to London since VE Day. All for the funeral of one girl. In 1981, she had waved from a glass coach. This time, the Queen's immaculate horses bore her along in a solid oak casket.

Neither, this time, was there drunken, happy singing outside Buckingham Palace. Just whispered conversations and muffled sobbing. People comforted strangers because, as Diana's friend Peter Settelen told me: "Diana's gift was to connect us, one to another, emotionally." No funeral, no event in history could be compared to Diana's send-off. The only fitting description was the official one: a unique service for a unique person. Diana's singularity was reflected by the hotchpotch of society that invaded Westminster Abbey. From the famous and powerful to the obscure and down-trodden. Invitations to the service were hastily dispatched, largely based on Diana's eclectic Christmas card list. Thus guests trooping into the Abbey evoked a confused Oscar Night: actors and pop stars in black. Psychic healers mingling with world leaders. Europe's aristocracy and glitterati rubbing black silk shoulders with nobodies whose claim to worth on that day – the affection of a Princess – made them somebodies.

We had seen Diana in jeans, bathing suits and Dior gowns. Nothing prepared us for the first gut-wrenching sight of her coffin draped in the Royal Standard. Outside Kensington Palace, a woman onlooker wailed. But apart

WE GIVE THANKS FOR THE LIFE OF A WOMAN I AM SO PROUD TO BE ABLE TO CALL MY SISTER THE UNIQUE·THE COMPLEX·THE EXTRAORDINARY & IRREPLACEABLE DIANA·WHOSE BEAUTY BOTH INTERNAL & EXTERNAL WILL NEVER BE EXTINGUISHED FROM OUR MINDS
Charles 9th Earl Spencer ·6th Sept 1997

NOTHING BRINGS ME MORE HAPPINESS THAN TRYING TO HELP THE MOST VULNERABLE PEOPLE IN SOCIETY·IT IS A GOAL AND AN ESSENTIAL PART OF MY LIFE·A KIND OF DESTINY·WHOEVER IS IN DISTRESS CAN CALL ON ME I WILL COME RUNNING WHEREVER THEY ARE
Diana Princess of Wales ·June 1997

Two memorial plaques at Althorp, Diana's birthplace, immortalise her words and those of her brother Charles. The Earl's speech during the funeral service in Westminster Abbey was spontaneously applauded by the crowd outside.

from the clopping of hooves and a mourning bell that chimed every minute, silence prevailed during the gun carriage's two-mile journey. Seeing how jauntily the white lilies bobbed atop the coffin, I thought of how Diana loved to dance. When her partners pegged out at parties, she would happily bop on alone. Today she had no partner, but we would not let her be alone.

The procession made its slow way to Buckingham Palace. Here 2.5 billion television viewers saw something barely visible to the crowd: one Majesty and a gathering of Royal Highnesses bowed their heads to the woman they had stripped of a royal title a year before. Angered that the Windsors had holed themselves up in Scotland for most of the grieving week, the crowds needed pacifying. Head-bows and a Union Jack which was lowered on the Palace flagstaff helped, though many saw such gestures as too little, too late. They said they wanted a warmer, more touchable Monarchy. More like Diana.

Prince William, Prince Harry, Prince Charles and Prince Philip waited with Earl Spencer at St James's Palace. The erect bearing of the two older Windsors bespoke their military training. The slumped shoulders of Diana's two sons spoke achingly of their grief. For Charles and his father – both vilified in Diana's melodrama – the walk behind the cortège probably took as much courage as they possessed. Sentimentally, Charles chose to wear a blue suit Diana had chosen for him in happier days. With a pat on the shoulder here and there for the boys, the five men somehow completed their longest, most silent mile. Harry's shorter legs required an occasional extra hop to keep pace. Prince William did not once raise his gaze from the road.

Of the ordeal beside his nephews, Charles Spencer later said: "It was harrowing . . . I was walking down a tunnel of grief. I would have been in tears if (the boys) hadn't been there and being a generation senior to them, I couldn't cry if they weren't. My admiration for those two boys is without bounds now. It's the most amazing display of courage that I'll ever see."

Boldly in the royal wake came a raggle-taggle army of representatives of the charities Diana had befriended. Some rolled in wheelchairs or swung on crutches. Many wore the T-shirt logos of their charities. In their presence that day, they were more relevant than all the Tom Cruises and Hillary Clintons, who simply knew her as a Princess. The charity people knew Diana as a flesh-and-blood angel who touched them in their need.

Meanwhile the Spencers had arrived as a unified force at the Abbey. Knowing in advance that Charles Spencer's eulogy would soon shatter the traditions of these very walls, there was a defiance in the family's march to

The Queen speaks live to the nation on TV after the public reaction to the Royal Family's apparent lack of emotion over Diana's death. (Above) Another placatory gesture? The Union Jack flies at half-mast over Buckingham Palace.

pews that would squarely face the Windsors. Matriarch Mrs Shand Kydd wore more jewellery than is *de rigeur* for a funeral but there was a message in each piece. In this ancient Anglican stronghold, the elaborate cross advertised her Catholicism. The multi-layered pearls were her late daughter's trademark. The pearl and diamond earrings had been borrowed by Diana on her wedding day. Mrs Shand Kydd also wore the Princess' own funeral hat, last used when Johnny Spencer died in 1992.

In eerie silence, the funeral cortège reached Westminster Abbey. Here twelve Welsh guards shouldered the casket and shuffled under its 560 pounds to the catafalque between the Spencers and the Windsors. Away from the cameras at last, the two families faced each other like black and white chess pieces. William shielded his face with one hand and stayed relatively poised until Elton John's voice rasped the first lines of "Candle in the Wind". Then the eldest son wept uncontrollably, Harry buried his head in his hands. Charles seemed agitated and the Queen Mother deathly pale. The "unique service" for a pop princess was complete with a roaring ovation for the song from those watching on giant screens in Hyde Park.

This release of tension changed the throng's mood from sombre to celebrating. Though the senior Windsors flinched during Earl Spencer's "We your blood family" eulogy, all of Hyde Park rose to its feet and applauded its barbed content. Like a tidal wave, the applause swept along the funeral route

The memorial to the Princess which her brother Charles has created at Althorp. (Above) The mock Greek temple topped by a cross as Diana's brother wanted to eliminate any semblance of paganism. (Facing page) The tiny central island in the lake at Althorp hosts this sculptured urn, surmounted by a flame. It does not mark Diana's grave – very few know its exact location.

and into the Abbey itself, where even the young Princes found themselves clapping. As the coffin was loaded into the hearse for Diana's slow return for burial at Althorp, the grief of the multitudes seemed to lift. From here on, they would celebrate their Princess.

As they had done during her life, people farewelled her while hardly able to let go. But for every one of the 77 miles, they forestalled the emptiness by tossing flowers in her path and, yes, applauding her for the happiness she brought them. At Althorp's gates, the incredible soap opera was over forever. For sixteen roller-coaster years, it had been Diana's world. We, the billions of people whom she fascinated, were fortunate to have lived in it at at the same time. Our last glimpse of her was the flag-draped casket, as the hearse headed for her peaceful island and for a grave whose exact location would be secret. Then the cameras went dark. The kettle was on and we could turn the television off.

The most touching tribute of all. The card from Diana's sons, William and Harry, on her coffin.

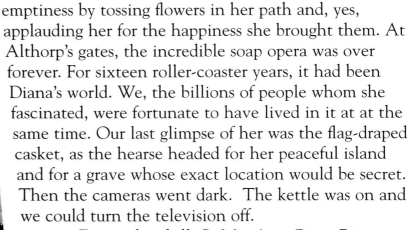

From a low hill, St Mary's at Great Brington overlooks Althorp and its oval lake. The little church holds the remains and, no doubt, the secrets of 20 generations of Spencers. In 1992, Diana and her siblings placed the ashes of their father beneath the flagstones of the family vault. Her own will said she wished to be buried. So, as only cremated remains can be interred in the vault, burial excluded her from this inner sanctum. Nevertheless, one feels her spirit in the Spencer pews, where she must have often knelt as a teenager. Here she rattled her half-crown in the collection plate, happily sang her favourite hymns and prayed for things that mattered to a "nice quiet country girl" before her whole world turned crazy.

And away from the holiday atmosphere of Charles Spencer's Dianaville, this was where I said my prayer. That wherever she lies, the Princess rests peacefully. That she knows her life really mattered to us and that we will eventually let her go.